Praise for *It's Not Out There*

'It's not out there' is a fabulous way to pause and reflect on the choices we make in our lives as we often hurtle through them. I found myself inwardly gulping as I recognized so much of what Danapriya talks to us about. His writing style is instantly accessible, so 'just like me', so relatable. I'd heartily recommend it to anyone that is ripe for change but a little uncertain which direction to take. – **Paul Brickel**, founder of Team Talk Hospitality

The path of love is bound up with sorrow, the path of beauty with loss. Danapriya's feeling for the deep truth of this – of how to live through and past it – is evident from his own story. His is a life changed by struggle and by his discovery of the Dharma as a pole star for love and the down-to-earth, everyday work that lets it shine. – **Candradasa**, Director of The Buddhist Centre Online

Bravo Danapriya! You have managed to put down concisely yet amusingly the Complete guide to a more Complete Life. I wish I had had access to this book whilst still practising as a GP, it could help so very many sufferers. And I wish I had had it when younger and suffering the vagaries of life myself. The text is dense and requires slow, contemplative reading, which is a virtue in itself: it is well worth putting in the time and concentration to read, mark, learn, and inwardly di

– **Dr Ingrid Dodd**, retired GP an

T0272956

Written in simple, down-to-earth language, *It's Not Out There* is brimming with practical wisdom. Positive and encouraging, Danapriya shares ways to help anyone who wants to change their life and find greater happiness and fulfilment. – **Dr Paramabandhu Groves**, co-author of *Eight Step Recovery: Using the Buddha's Teachings to Overcome Addiction*

Danapriya has written a little gem of a book. *It's Not Out There* is concise, straightforward, engaging, accessible, and eminently practical. A starter-kit for making the most of your life. – **Maitreyabandhu**, author of *Life with Full Attention* and *The Journey and the Guide*

This is a very practical book that can help anyone attempting to navigate life's unpredictable currents without capsizing or being blown off course. The ideas are easy to grasp and Danapriya gives a wealth of useful advice about how to put them into practice. The simplicity of how to stop, look, sense, and listen is a message that the world desperately needs at the moment. I'm trying to practise it myself. – **Manidhara** (Graham Titus), Buddhist musician

This thoughtful book will help you reassess how to live your best life. Using techniques of mindfulness Danapriya explains how to reap the enjoyment from everyday moments. In the manic pace of today's world he helps provide a much-needed space for reflection. – **Lindsay Powell**

Danapriya communicates his hard-won wisdom and love in a way that is simple and easy to follow, yet somehow the simplicity makes it all the more challenging. Each short chapter prompted me to ask myself: what more could I be doing to enrich my life and the lives of others? We get some good pointers for the journey. – **Satyadasa**, founder of Standing Body Health and Buddhist Tutor at Eton College

Reading this book is like having a conversation with a wise friend – someone who doesn't just talk at you but who is interested in your thoughts and experience, too. Buy one for everyone you know who is serious about life and how to live it well. – **Subhadramati**, author of *Not About Being Good*

'It's not out there, it's here' is a timely reminder of how we all shape our own lives. Danapriya has given us a gentle yet provocative, personal yet universal, straightforward yet tender account of what it means to be human and the choices and responsibilities that go with it. He gives us the benefit of his years of experience as a Buddhist practitioner to give us frank, accessible insights into the ways we choose or not to live meaningful and fulfilling lives. At times powerfully honest, Danapriya lays it all out on the dinner table in front of us, and in so doing invites us to fully contemplate the meals we are eating and the diet we are choosing. – **Paul Swift**, psychotherapist

Reading this book is like having a super-encouraging and wise friend who really believes in you and wants you to be the best you can possibly be! – **Vajragupta**, Buddhist teacher and writer, author of *Buddhism: Tools for Living Your Life*

It's Not Out There

It's Not Out There

How to See Differently and Live an Extraordinary, Ordinary Life

Danapriya

(w) indhorse Publications

Windhorse Publications
info@windhorsepublications.com
windhorsepublications.com

Typesetting and layout by Tarajyoti
Cover design by Katarzyna Manecka
Printed by Bell & Bain Ltd, Glasgow

British Library Cataloguing in Publication Data:
A catalogue record for this book is available from the British Library.

ISBN: 978-1-911407-59-1

Contents

Contents

About the author

Danapriya, born Ian Dixon in 1959, has been involved in personal growth and healing work for over three decades. He is a fully qualified acupuncturist, having studied at the College of Integrated Chinese Medicine from 1993 to 1996, and has been in private practice ever since. He has also studied cognitive behavioural therapy (CBT) and neuro-linguistic programming (NLP).

On being ordained into the Triratna Buddhist Order in 2001 he was given the name Danapriya, meaning 'one who loves giving'. He lived at the London Buddhist Centre for nine years before moving to Deal in Kent, UK, where he set up the Deal Buddhist Group. He was chair of the group for eleven years, stepping down from the role in 2018. Over the years Danapriya has led many retreats and taught hundreds of people to meditate.

Danapriya now leads courses in positive thinking and meditation, as well as running a counselling business called TLC (*Talking Listening Clarity*). *It's Not Out There* is his first book. For Danapriya's led meditations outlined in this book as well as more information on his counselling see www.danapriya.org.

Acknowledgements

First of all I want to thank my Mum and Dad, Jan and Alan, who gave birth to me, without which none of this rich life would be possible. I also want to acknowledge and thank a few of the many teachers who have shared gifts of wisdom and encouragement with me. Ratnaghosha, who ordained me and gave me the name Danapriya – one who loves giving. He is the person I look to most for life's guidance. He gave me the confidence to write this book. Manidhara, who read the manuscript as it appeared and helped shape my slightly interesting use of English. Priyananda, who gave me the opportunity for this book to be published. And Dhiramuni and Cynthia, who edited the manuscript so thoughtfully and kindly, from whom I felt educated in the art of writing.

Publisher's acknowledgements

Windhorse Publications wishes to gratefully acknowledge a grant from the Triratna European Chairs' Assembly Fund and the Future Dharma Fund towards the production of this book.

Windhorse Publications also wishes to gratefully acknowledge and thank the individual donors who gave to the book's production via our 'Sponsor-a-book' campaign.

Foreword by Dhiramuni

What sort of person do you want to be? How do you want to live your life? Are you happy with the choices you make – about how you behave, the friends you choose, even how you spend your time? When something troubles you, do you blame other people and outside events? Is it always someone else's fault?

In this clear, accessible book Danapriya asks: 'Who is running your mind?'

The answer, of course, is you – and you have a choice at all times. You can *choose* to focus on the more positive aspects of your life, in particular your relationships with others and with yourself, and to develop those qualities. Or you can *choose* to stay in the same old negative mindset, blaming everybody and everything else for what befalls you. In so doing you are denying yourself the transformative possibilities that can result from developing an open, receptive, positive heart.

Danapriya is an ordained Buddhist and an experienced teacher of the Dharma (as we call the teachings of the Buddha) and of meditation. In this potentially life-changing book he has used plain, everyday language almost completely free of 'Buddhist' terminology to create a guide for living your life more joyfully and skilfully. Much of what he has to say is based on his own experiences as a practising Buddhist. If what he writes seems simple and straightforward, that's because it is! And he has a gift for offering imaginative anecdotes or observations, usually from his own experience, to illustrate a point.

The way to happiness and contentment, Danapriya writes, lies within ourselves, in our heart, mind, and body. Thus, to quote the title of the book, the way forward is 'not out *there'* – it's *here*. By calling one of the early chapters in the book 'It's never not now', he's very clear where and when the action must take place. To quote a key Buddhist teaching, what we dwell on we become – what we turn our minds to influences our thinking and our behaviour.

Above all else, *It's Not Out There* is a practical handbook for living our lives more skilfully. As the reader you'll find some parts speak to you particularly strongly. For me, one that resonated sharply was the need to be generous in *receiving* generosity from others. In New Zealand, where I live, it's not uncommon for people to decline acts of generosity from others, saying something like, 'Oh, it's OK, don't worry,' or, 'don't go to any trouble,' in effect denying the other person the opportunity to be generous. Danapriya encourages us to try to *receive* generosity with a generous and receptive heart. 'It keeps the flow of generosity going,' he says.

This is just a snippet of the great riches contained in this book. It's a cliché, but following Danapriya's insights really *could* change your life – if you open yourself to the possibility.

Dhiramuni
Editor, former publisher
Teacher, Auckland Buddhist Centre

Introduction

It's not out there, it's here

So often we are looking outside ourselves for happiness, love, contentment, and more, but it's not out there. 'It' – happiness, love, contentment, and more – is within us. We are stuffed full of these qualities and more. When we wake up to this fact, what is out there becomes amazing.

I am Danapriya, and, like you, I have been on a life's journey with many experiences; many joyful, some painful, and lots of neutral, 'ordinary' days. This book enables us to see clearly how we make our pain more painful, and that we really don't need to; how we can make our ordinary times extraordinary, and our joyful times even more so.

Through the first thirty years of my life I was looking out there for happiness, success, love, and more. My health stopped me in my tracks at thirty years old; the first chapter tells the story. Since that event of thirty years ago I have been looking inside myself and life has become more vivid, joyful, and extraordinary.

With hindsight, I can see that when I was a child, nature and quiet connected me to something beautiful and awesome happening in the universe. Later I described myself as a Christian, then a Spiritualist, and now I am a Buddhist, all of which have helped me to make some sense of life, some sense of meaning, faith, and the beyond, while holding the fact that none of us knows what is actually going on.

I lived the first fifteen years of my life in a stable, loving family, which then blasted apart. I made myself very independent, and a successful businessman, travelling the world extensively. Then I became ill for eight years. I have lived in a Buddhist community for nine years, where I trained to be ordained, which happened in 2001. I have founded and run a successful Buddhist group for eleven years, as well as practising as a Traditional Chinese Acupuncturist since 1995. I have been on hundreds of retreats both in the UK and abroad. The longest retreat was four months. Therefore, I bring all of this diverse life experience, both spiritual and worldly, to this book.

Here I share many of my personal experiences and what I have learnt from my many teachers and friends, and from many events, courses, wisdoms, and spiritual traditions. These have shown me how I so easily trip myself up by my thoughts, my views, and my habits. By really taking time, stopping, looking, feeling, and listening, I have gained a new level of awareness that has radically and positively shifted the way I understand things. This has totally enhanced my whole life, and I greatly want to share all I have learnt with you and others. So here it is, my first book.

People who have read this book so far have said how accessible it is, what an easy read, yet how profound, and how relatable it is to their life. *It's Not Out There* is for anyone, from any walk of life, who wants to suffer less, and to live their life so it enriches all aspects of being human. This book is about seeing the reality of our human predicament, discarding all the illusions that create unnecessary pain for ourselves and others. With the help of this book you can make your life extraordinary.

It's Not Out There **and connecting online**

I have decided that my next decade will be dedicated to sharing what I have been given. I have been given teachings from so many people from many walks of life. Those teachings have positively helped me, and when I benefit, the natural human urge is to want to share them, as widely as possible. Therefore, I have a new website for this new decade, showing the ways I am sharing. Do take a look: www.danapriya.org.

Through the following chapters I ask you questions to reflect on. If you would like to share your thoughts with me, or ask any questions, I would love to hear from you via the website.

1

Even pain can bring blessings

It may seem strange to start this book with the subject of pain. But through all my years of talking with and helping people I have learnt that most personal growth journeys start with some pain, whether the pain of physical illness, emotional trauma, the death of someone close, being made redundant, or several of life's painful events. We don't change our habits very easily, even though they may be uncomfortable. More than anything else, pain is the one thing that can move us to change.

Suddenly at the age of thirty my energy disappeared. It felt like I had been unplugged from the mains. The date was Sunday 25 March 1990. Until that day most people would have looked at my life and said, 'Danapriya's made it, what a good life he has' (although I was not yet Danapriya). I had a great partner. We had a home in London and one in Brighton. I was general manager of a business travel company in London's Mayfair district, and travelled extensively. I had many friends, went to lots of parties, the theatre, and exhibitions, generally having what I thought was a good life.

Yes, my life was good, but was it the life I was meant to be living? Was it my life, or the life I thought I should be living because of how I was told to live by others – parents, teachers, society, culture? I don't remember ever stopping and asking, 'What do I want to do? What sort of life do I want to live?' Sort of blindly I had just done the next thing. One day my body said, 'STOP!' I became bedbound for thirteen months, then unable to leave my flat for about another eight months.

Although my life looked like I had made it in a worldly sense, my body had other ideas. Suddenly I was being looked after, luckily so very well by my partner, family, and friends, certainly they were all a great blessing. I had lost my job: my employer paid me for three months, then I needed to claim sickness benefits. I had to sell my London flat and live in my partner's flat in Brighton. My energy felt close to zero. I cried a lot during those early months, although I don't remember being unhappy; I think the crying was a relief from holding up a pretence that I had no idea I was holding. After nine months, having been tested for many illnesses by the National Health Service (NHS), I was diagnosed with Myalgic Encephalomyelitis (ME): basically extreme fatigue.

With hindsight, however, my own diagnosis would be emotional exhaustion. After a very loving, stable childhood, when I was fifteen my Mum left the family home, which was a total shock. Two years later my Dad threw me out of home because his new wife did not want to look after his children. These two events felt like rejections, and I think I then went at life, people-pleasing and trying to be a perfectionist, so that no one else ever rejected me again – and that's exhausting.

The NHS offered me antidepressants, and although I had been very upset in the early months after having lost my good health, energy, job, and home, I was not depressed. I was appropriately and healthily sad for my change of circumstances. After about a year of resting my body, I started reading my first personal growth book, *Feel the Fear and Do It Anyway*, by Susan Jeffers. This began my search. How did I want to spend this precious life of mine?

Western medicine was unable to help with ME at that time, having only recently labelled the illness as such. I started to look for alternatives. My dear friend Glen was a Spiritualist, and he suggested that I try spiritual healing. At this point I was willing to try anything. My partner wrote to the National Federation of Spiritual Healers (NFSH) to see if there was a healer in our area.

A few days later, I woke to a beautiful, blue-sky December morning. The sun was shining into the window of our second-floor flat, which I had not left on my own since arriving there about fourteen months earlier. Normally I waited for my partner to come home in the evening to bring up the mail from the ground-floor postbox, but on this day I felt drawn to go downstairs and collect the mail. There were two letters for me. I stood looking out of the main front door at the beautiful day. There is a street opposite called West Hill Street with lovely, white-painted houses which I have always liked. I walked out of the front door and up West Hill Street. After about twenty-five metres I felt absolutely exhausted and wondered how I was going to get back home. I sat on a house wall in the sunshine, and opened the first letter, which was from the NFSH. The letter said there was a healer in our area, and that they lived at 25 West Hill Street. I was sitting on the wall of 25 West Hill Street!

This moment has been of great significance to me. I felt guided that day. The moment of noticing that I was sitting exactly where I needed to be in West Hill Street helped me to realize that if I can get myself out of the way then I am guided by something. I don't know what, but it's been so kind to me – it's a delightful mystery. I know I need to listen to my inner world and mostly ignore the outer world. In the quiet, if I leave space to listen and see the coincidences and signs, I hear, feel, and sense my true direction.

If someone had said to me when I was twenty-nine, 'Next year you will lose your energy, job, and home', I would not have believed them. I would have been very scared of any one of those things happening. Yet they did happen and became the biggest blessing in my life. I had to stop, look, feel, and listen to the deeper voices and currents within, and ask questions:

What do I want to do with this precious life of mine?
How do I want to use my energy?
How do I want to manifest in this world?

Not, how do I think others want me to be? Or, what do others think I should do? Rather –

Truly, who am I?
How can I let my truth live?
How can I be the best human being?

Listen deeply and you will know. You don't have to wait for pain or tragedy, you can stop right now and look within.

Generally, we don't stop. We stay with discomfort – which may be, for example, a job we dislike that we go to day in, day out; week in, week out; year in, year out. We do things that are uncomfortable that we don't like, 'but', we say, 'but this', 'but that', any excuse not to let ourselves be free of the underlying pain. We don't like change. Or do we? Change is the focus of Chapter 6.

We stay in relationships that are past their sell-by date. We may talk to our friends about the relationship, but do we really talk to our partner and explore ways to change, so we can help one another enjoy our lives? Or instead do we suffer in silence and pretend?

I believe we often act and pretend. We don't even know we are doing this because we have not yet worked out what we are meant to be doing in this lifetime. We act, pretend, do what we think we should, or what we think others think we should, even though that's an illusion, because we have not even asked the others what they think we should do. We have guessed, and we could be wrong. To live this way is only half a life, not a fully lived and vitally meaningful life, where we make every moment count. Where we savour the beautiful. Where we leave a wonderful perfume in our wake.

The pain in my life has brought change and blessings. Had the painful experiences and events not happened I would not have lived and be living the rich, precious life that I live now. The pain has helped me to develop compassion and empathy for myself and others, helped me to 'put myself in others' shoes', and be grateful for all the blessings of my life.

This book covers a lot of the fertile ground that helps you live the life you are here for. Stop, look, feel, and listen, you are so worth it, you matter.

2

It's never not now

Many people miss much of their lives because they are lost in thought, whether about the future or the past. We crave for an experience that is to come, such as the weekend, a holiday, retirement, food, and, and … . I imagine this resonates with you, even if you are wishing or hoping for different things. Or we can be ruminating over the past, remembering events that have already happened, worrying about ways we acted, or getting angry about the ways others have treated us. This is all in the past.

When we choose either thoughts of the future or of the past we miss our life now. It's *never* not now. All those hopes for the future – when the future arrives, it *is* now, and guess what? We miss that hoped-for event because we are wishing for another experience in the future, or dwelling in the past. So we miss our life because our life only happens *now.* There is nothing ten minutes ago or twenty years ago and there is nothing in two hours' or five years' time. Our life can only be lived now. You may have noticed I said *choose* our thoughts, because what we think about is a *choice*, and what we dwell on we become.

In other words, I have learnt that what we *choose* to think about, or dwell on, we become. If we dwell on positive aspects of life, positive aspects of ourselves, or the positive qualities of others, we become happier, brighter, and more positive in all our relationships with people and with ourselves. Whereas if we dwell on negative thoughts, events, or conversations, then this certainly doesn't cheer us up. Rather, such dwelling creates a lot of tension in our body, mind, and emotions, which will in fact be the cause of 'dis-ease'.

Generally speaking, what we give out into the world we get back; we are mirrored by others. We can choose what we dwell on. I often hear friends and family say, 'That's not possible, I can't change!' The truth is we can't *not* change; we *are* change, we are in process, we are ageing all the time, our thoughts are changing all the time, our emotions change, our hair grows and falls out, our nails grow and we cut them, our skin dries and flakes into household dust. Some of these things we are unable to stop. But we *can* change what we think, how we act, and what we say.

So here are some questions:

Who is running your mind?
Who is in control of your actions?
Who makes the words come out of your mouth?

When we speak we can be kind or unkind. We can be mean or complimentary. And when we act we can act generously or harshly. *You* are in charge. Ideally, *you* need to take full responsibility for *your* life, firstly by seeing what happens *now*, then by assessing if that is helpful. If not, *change* – decide who you want to become. If you think that's impossible, keep reading and I will give you some guidelines how to achieve positive change.

What perfume do you want to leave in your wake?
What would you like people to say about you?

To feel really alive, and to feel life as it is happening, we need to be present *now*. You are a work of art that you are continuously creating. Because it's never not now, the opportunity is ever-present; you just need to *choose* to be here now. If you are here now you can tune in deeply to all your senses and feelings; to what you are seeing, smelling, tasting, and touching; to what emotion is present, and what thoughts you are having. Our senses are always communicating with us, always rich with life as it is happening. To make the most out of our life it's essential to be here *now* in order to receive the communication. Then we have absolutely all the information we need to make wise choices about how to be happy and content in ourselves, and in all our relationships.

I was out walking yesterday evening and I purposely left my mobile phone at home. I just made a choice not to be distracted from walking in nature. I strolled along the seafront, the moon was high and bright in a darkening blue sky. I stopped and looked up and felt the moment. I felt the slight cold of the evening breeze on my face. My body felt calmer and was tingling with the awesome sight of the moon hanging up there, shining. Had I been lost in future or past thoughts, it's likely I would not have noticed the moon at all. I noticed the sea's calmness after the gales of the last few days, and that the tide was out. I watched a few lapping waves and some seagulls floating on the surface. I was enjoying the simplicity and wonder of each moment.

I walked along the promenade to a place where there is an open view to the west. The sun was setting over the golf course; the lake there looked like a mirror reflecting the setting sun, while various birds made their evening calls. I was there in this magical moment, this moment which only exists if I am present *now*.

Walking back, I passed some people. I had a choice to say, 'Good evening', or to ignore them. I chose to speak, to give a kind word and acknowledge other human beings. In my experience it always lifts my spirit when I connect with others. I could have ignored them, yet I have noticed when I have done this in the past, I tend to think 'Miserable so-and-sos, why didn't they speak?' But that is not me taking responsibility for my actions and choices. It's not helpful, ever, to blame anyone else for anything. Your internal state is your choice. So I noticed that by speaking to the people I passed I felt more positive, and by not speaking it would have created negativity in my thoughts. This awareness has helped me create a habit of having the courage to speak to strangers, which is an expression of being kind, and which hopefully brightens their and my day.

Be here *now* and your life gets a whole lot better. You then learn to make wiser choices.

3

We live such rich lives

We live such rich lives due to thousands or probably millions of people doing things for us. People we will never meet – the people who grow our food, for instance. I don't know how many people were involved in my being able to eat my breakfast this morning: the oats were grown and harvested, then transported in a vehicle; many people were involved in making that vehicle, sourcing the fuel, building the roads; the oats were packaged and put on the shelves of my local supermarket; the supermarket was built by yet other human beings, it was designed by someone, checkout machines were there for me to pay at, and the money has been printed; I needed clothes to keep me warm for walking to the supermarket to be able to buy the oats I ate for breakfast.

In fact, I have no idea how many people are involved in my being able to have oats for breakfast, but it's certainly a lot! You may like to reflect on all the people and conditions that made your meal possible, and then allow to arise a sense of gratitude towards them. I hope you are developing a sense of just how connected we are to other people, most of whom we don't know and may never meet. I thank you. I thank you so much for helping me live such a rich life.

I was just talking about the oats. For breakfast today I also had flaxseeds, ground almonds, soya milk, blueberries, an apple, and red bush tea. There was also my bowl, spoon, and mug; the saucepan I cooked the porridge in; the water, the cooker, the kettle, the kitchen, and so on, and on. If we need a doctor or a hospital, a train or a bus, an airport or a station, there they are, with people waiting to help, to drive or to do whatever is needed to help us live such rich lives. If we google something, the answers 'magically' appear; of course, some-one put them there, and thousands of people would have been involved with the technology that enabled the words to appear on our wireless, handheld electronic device. Is that magic, or human beings?

Whenever I remember that I am helped by so many, gratitude arises in my heart. It helps me feel so positive towards strangers, towards people just like me. They have their joys, their fears, they love and are loved, they experience anxiety, they have their doubts, they get angry, and are kind. We are all so very much the same deep down, yet we manifest uniquely through our choice of thoughts, words, and actions, which sculpt who we are at this moment. By choosing how we see the world, a huge difference is made to our inner world, and therefore to how we act.

Noticing that I can't live my life without millions of others doing things for me helps me not feel alone. I feel connected and have much gratitude in my heart. Also, I see that these people are just like me. They want to be loved, they love, they want to feel safe, have a home, have food, and a sense of happiness and achievement. All this leads to contentment.

As we travel around the planet, most of the people we see we don't know. Some may be familiar, in that we may see them regularly, such as our neighbours and the people who serve us in shops, whereas others are totally new to us, and we may find we experience a subtle level of fear or suspicion in relation to them. We can then tense slightly and be on our guard. All this creates 'dis-ease' within us. Instead, we could reflect on how these people who are unknown to us may be doing something which helps us live our life more richly. Then we will feel a connection with them and the fear can dissolve.

Fear, of course, is useful in situations that are potentially threatening. There are some streets in some cities where I would not walk in the early hours of a Saturday or a Sunday morning. Yet most streets and places are probably non-threatening. The fear is created in our own minds and leads to limiting our lives and hearts. It is possible to feel at ease within ourselves, and even with strangers, who, if we knew them, might even become good friends.

My teacher Sangharakshita says, 'I believe that humanity is basically one. I believe that it is possible for any human being to communicate with any other human being, to feel for any other human being, to be friends with any other human being. This is what I truly and deeply believe.' (These lines are in his book *Living with Kindness*.) Human beings don't seem to accept difference very readily. This is tragic, because the reality is that we are *all* different, we are *all* unique, we *all* have our very own story and journey. Our different cultures, nationalities, likes or dislikes, and our different personalities – all give our world the amazing richness of variety, colour, fascination, and interest. If we were all the same, life would indeed be so very dull. For a happy, contented life we need to accept difference and not fight it; we need to be interested in and accept the joy of difference. We are then dealing with how things are – with truth. Then life gets so much easier, and joy can flood in.

Reflecting on gratitude and on connection with others will enhance our experience. It will help us to realize that the richness of our lives, with all the extraordinary choices at our disposal, is only possible because of all those wonderful, unique people whom we may not know. But I thank whoever they are so very much, from the bottom of my heart.

4

It's not out there

So exactly *what* is not out there? We all seem to have an inbuilt tendency to look for something outside ourselves – outside our heart, mind, and body – that will make us happy, contented, and satisfied.

We may look for a partner who will fulfil our romantic dreams but also make us feel safe and secure by looking after us. We may talk of our 'other half', although personally I dislike this phrase. If I have a partner, I would like them to be a whole person, not half a person. Likewise, I would like to be a whole person myself, not just a half.

It is so easy to give our true selves away when in a relationship. This doesn't have to be the case. We can be two whole individuals relating fully and wholeheartedly from the truth of ourselves, which will lead to far more happiness for both partners. We would then be leading full and individual lives, sharing our love and supporting each other in who each of us is truly becoming. We would then be who we want to be without the chains of trying to fit ourselves into a certain shape for our partner.

Or we may look to material things, such as cars, clothes,

places to live, holidays, or music, to make us feel happy, contented, satisfied. There is absolutely no problem at all with having things, going on holiday, listening to music, or even playing computer games – but if we are looking to get more from them than they can give, we will always be disappointed.

We may go shopping, looking to buy something new which will make us feel better, more complete, and return home with the latest mobile phone. We've got the best one, in its amazing box and bag. We play with it, and it does seem to satisfy us for a while. Then slowly it becomes just another everyday object. Later on we may be at the cinema and see an advertisement for the latest mobile phone model just released. The advertisement gets the message across very strongly that the new model is even better than the one we already have. Then we may be dissatisfied with the mobile phone we have, we may even feel not good enough. If so, the only way to feel better, it seems, is to have the latest model, which costs more than we can comfortably afford. This all creates stress, pressure, and unhappiness. We might feel we have to work extra hours to obtain the object which we think is going to complete us and make us happier.

Does this pattern of behaviour sound familiar? The idea about feeling better with the new mobile phone is an illusion, a result of marketing and advertising. The same illusion keeps the world of economic growth spinning, making banks and credit card companies wealthy, creating stress, anxiety, and sleepless nights for many consumers. Such a cycle will never complete us or make us happy and content.

Such a cycle will also cause us to suffer. Happiness is not out there. So where is it? It's in our being, in our heart, mind, and body. We find happiness and contentment in our spirit, in knowing ourselves, in seeing things as they really are.

We all have a tendency to be blinded by peer pressure, by views that have been passed down to us from parents, teachers, newspapers, and from the whole world around us, views that it's important to check out for ourselves. I encourage you to look deep inside your being, and ask:

Who am I?

Who do I wish to become during this lifetime?

We all have this precious gift of life. We are creating it at every moment with each action, thought, word, and emotion. We like to think we have full control of all of these, whereas much of the time we live on automatic pilot which will lead us astray. To live fully we need to be able to respond fully to life. To take responsibility for our life. There is no one to blame. If we blame others or ourselves we just create pain for ourselves.

Getting to know our own mind and emotions is the key to our freedom. We begin to see how things really are. Then, knowing the truth, we can make wiser choices for ourselves and others, choices that truly express who we are and who we are becoming. We are a work of art that it is in our own hands to create at every moment. However, we need to get to know the raw material to be able to work well with it.

Looking honestly inside ourselves, on close inspection we will find that we are much better than we think, and also much worse. By taking hold of the reins of our life and making the changes which will lead to less stress and anxiety we will find inner contentment, simple joy, and peace, because these positive emotions have always been there. It's just that we have an ingrained habit of looking outside ourselves, out there. We can't change out there. We can't change others, but we can change ourselves and our responses to people and situations. We can always speak more kindly to ourselves and others. We can be content with who we are. If we can stop comparing ourselves with others we will be able to stop feeling we have to keep up with them, and with the world's clever way of getting us to spend more money.

When we are truly taking care of ourselves like this, we automatically take more care of others. Once we feel more complete inside, then we have more to give and to share: there is an abundance. This has nothing to do with material possessions or wealth. We can have a generous heart, a generous spirit, and a generous mind, and feel absolutely abundant, yet on a material level have very little. Or we can be mean-hearted, mean-spirited, and mean-minded, yet on a material level have absolutely everything. Which of us is happier? Materially speaking, the person who has more will have more to lose. They will have more to hold on to and so they will experience more stress and anxiety. It really doesn't matter how much we have or don't have. It's all to do with our inner world, with our inner sense of self, the degree to which we acknowledge and live from our inner riches, our inner wealth.

Get to know your inner riches and let them shine. Everyone will benefit. It's not out there.

Stop
Look
Feel
Listen

Your inner world has all the answers.

5

I don't have enough time

When I am teaching positive thinking and meditation courses, or seeing clients, I often hear people say, 'I don't have enough time.' Though understandable, this is definitely an illusion, a wrong view. If we are alive we do have time. We always have time. What matters is what we choose to do with our time and, most importantly, the mind we bring to everything. Are we present to the moment, or are we piling into our head a list of things to do, feeling overwhelmed and anxious, rather than enjoying this time, now?

As set out in Chapter 2, it's never not now. Now is both your life and your time. If you are aware enough to be here now with your body, with your emotions and mind in harmony, you will lead a spacious life, one which is time-rich instead of time-poor. It's the same life, but your experience feels totally different. When we see through the illusion of the words 'I never have enough time,' time slows down, and we experience having more of it.

Our main fear is that we won't get done all that we think we are supposed to do in order to feel all right. It so often comes back to 'I don't feel good enough,' or else the cultural conditioning of the 'overdoing it' work ethic. Society is continually strengthening this view by demanding more from people, by targets, personal reviews, and the expectation that we should work longer hours than we are paid for, or else we are not considered a 'good employee'. The fear is often a question of self-worth, and of not realizing what an amazing gift you are. Most of us want to be thought well of, to be respected for who we are, and have people who are proud of us. That's a healthy need. Unfortunately, the same need can easily tip over into us exerting a desperate amount of pressure on ourselves. Then our view of time is squeezed into the 'poverty mentality' of never having enough.

There has always been enough. Time is just time. It's very quiet, orderly, reliable, and just beautifully happening without anything needed from us. Ideally, we simply enjoy being alive in each moment, doing what we are doing as fully and calmly as possible. We don't even have to give time a thought, apart from being where we said we would be to help other people.

It's good to remember who it was that made that date to meet someone. To remember who said 'yes' to that job; or even to remember who is running your life, 'running' often being the operative word. You can so easily miss the blossom and the smiles as you rush through. Someone said to me years ago that I seemed to go through life with a hand on my back pushing me very hard, always trying to achieve, incessantly people-pleasing, doing so much in a day, multitasking, working late. They felt exhausted just watching me. I realized that the hand on my back was mine. I saw it was me doing the pushing, and that I could change that relentless force into a gentle, caring one: a hand which supported me and did not drive me so fast that I missed the joy as it passed.

Something in me woke up, then released and settled. The experience felt like a wave of clarity, like the sun coming out from behind dark clouds. Afterwards my shoulders relaxed, and I sighed. At that moment I wanted to live my life so differently – which now and again I have managed to do. But we don't change deep habits easily.

With the help of meditation, spiritual teachings, and more support from people further along the path of personal growth, my life now has a more calm and spacious feel to it. Yet I achieve just as much as I did before, if not more. It's all to do with my state of mind, my emotional view of myself, and the awareness of my physical body and breath in each moment. Awareness is the key to seeing through the self-imposed oppression of time. Time can't oppress. It's I who choose to oppress myself, through telling myself such stories as 'people won't love me if …', 'I will be told off if …', 'I will lose my job if …'. Such stories are not helpful to living a joyful, contented, and time-rich life.

When we stop and look at our relationship with time, we learn a lot about ourselves. I have friends who are usually late when meeting with me. They tend to be people who want to do 'just one last thing' before leaving home or work. They don't leave enough time for the journey to the meeting point, which in itself creates stress, stress that is actually self-created. Even if you are running late, believe it or not, you can still be relaxed and arrive calm! Admittedly, you will have taken up some of the other person's time, and not kept your word about the hour of meeting, but you can always make amends. However, if you see that this kind of lateness is a pattern, then it may be worth looking at why you keep doing that 'one last thing'?

I know that if I leave early to get to wherever I am going, I see more, feel more, and hear more. I enjoy the journey, the walk. I have some mental and emotional space to be fully aware and feel my life. Then I am ready for whatever I have chosen to do next – to be fully with my friend, for example. I feel more ready to laugh and relax, without the need for a few glasses of wine, beer, or gin to cast off the tension that previously I would have created.

Occasionally you may have noticed that time doesn't appear to last the same length for everything we do. An hour spent doing something we really enjoy can whizz by. An hour absorbed in something we are engaged with can fly past. Yet an hour spent on something we find boring can take what seems like forever, and doing something for an hour that we grudgingly said 'Yes' to can really drag. Why? As I get older I have also noticed that the months and years go by faster. Many people I know say the same thing. I wonder why this is. I am sure it has something to do with our perception of time and not with the clock.

Perception is the organization, identification, and interpretation of information which comes in through our senses, so we can represent and understand that information, as well as our environment. It depends on our senses what we, see, feel, hear, taste, smell, think, and emote, and these are all personal and unique to each moment. Each moment is therefore different and will feel shorter or longer depending on our degree of engagement with whatever we are doing. Or maybe we are just being....

When I do my daily meditation, some practices whizz by and others can seem to last forever, even though in both cases I have meditated for fifty minutes. My level of engagement, intention, and focus create my perception. I can choose to engage; to decide my intention and focus fully, or not. It's all my doing, the choices that I make. Any anxiety, tension, or pressure with regard to time happens precisely because I create it. The great freedom in knowing this is that once I see differently, I can choose differently. I am running my life. I have full responsibility. I can remove the oppression of time, allowing the clouds to part and the sun to shine, dissolving the shadows cast by the view that 'I never have enough time.'

6

I can't change

Life is change. Every moment is new. We are a process; we are born and so we die. We buy a new pair of shoes in great condition and then they wear out, or often these days we have bought another pair before our existing pair has worn out. Then our *taste* in shoes changes. In fact, our taste in anything can change. Our moods change several times a day; the weather, as we know, changes; the clouds are forever changing; our hair changes colour and falls out.

Everything is change. In spring the daffodils grow, flower, and die; then tulips do the same, then cherry blossoms. Every day we see change before our very eyes. Yet it's not uncommon for people to say, 'Oh, I can't change.' They suppose that they couldn't possibly learn to use a washing machine, cook a meal, paint a picture, use a smartphone, or learn a new language.

We greatly limit ourselves by what we choose to think. What is so special about *you* that you can't learn that new language; that you can't learn to swim, ride a horse, sing – or become computer literate? My ninety-five-year-old friend Diana uses her desktop computer and a tablet computer, orders things online, Skypes with friends around the world, and sends cards via email. We can always learn new skills, we can always change our mind. Remember: *what we dwell on we become.*

If you dwell on 'I can't' then you won't, but if you dwell on 'I can' then you will. Don't stay limited within the tight box that you have created for yourself. Step out into freedom, 'face the fear and do it anyway'. Fear is part of life, and we rarely experience any excitement or anything new without going beyond fear. For the most part the fear is mind-made by the stories we tell ourselves, and most often these stories are full of fear about what could go wrong. We will catastrophize everything if we are not careful. Change the story. It's as easy as that: change your mind.

Do you really need this unhelpful habit, when it's possible to stop? Remember that, in any case, you are already changing. Dance, join the gym, learn to meditate, go to Thailand, visit that neighbour. Take a risk and break out into a new and brighter world. Doing so is your choice. What, exactly, are you waiting for? Ask that person on a date, learn to sail, change your job, move house, get a dog. The list is endless, if you step out of your self-imposed limited world.

Who is running your life?
Who thinks your thoughts?

As long as what you do doesn't harm anyone, just do it. There is no good choice or bad choice, there is just learning, gaining experience; there is just the choice that can expand what is possible for you.

What prevents us from taking a risk? We often decide whether we like something before we have tried it. Take food, for instance: knowing from experience that all those spices don't agree with my digestion, I don't eat Thai food, but if you have never tried it, you don't actually know whether you would like it or not. I tried olives when I was younger and didn't like them at all, so I decided there and then that I was someone who didn't like olives. I didn't eat them again for years, until someone encouraged me to try one. Guess what? Now I like olives! We change.

Of course, olives are not too serious a matter. The consequences for our spiritual lives may be a lot more serious. Maybe in the past you had a difficult relationship with religion, and you decided that there is no meaning in it, in God or whatever. This is absolutely fine, but may mean that you rule out any form of spiritual teaching, or faith, or any other dimension existing in our unending universe. It's also likely that you have not investigated the full range of spiritual teachings, let alone the mysteries of the universe! As we all know, when life gets difficult – which it always does at some point – there is suffering. It's just how things are.

So what do we do with suffering? When life turns tricky my experience has shown that I need to take a bigger perspective, a sense of a bigger dimension to help me through – not only to help me through the difficult times but to enhance my whole life.

I am a Buddhist. I used to be a Spiritualist, and before that I was christened into the Church of England by my parents. At present I live wholeheartedly as a Buddhist. So far what I have experienced has convinced me that Buddhism makes complete sense, it helps my life enormously and requires no blind belief. *But* I am also open to the possibility of something else I don't yet know about. There may be something even more helpful. Now I'm not trying to persuade anyone to convert to Buddhism. What I *am* encouraging you to do is to explore your soul, the spiritual aspect of your nature. In a way, you are doing it now by reading this book. Thank you, I hope it helps.

I am someone you would certainly not have called cultured; by 'cultured' I mean someone who read poetry, listened to classical music, or went to the opera, the ballet, or to art galleries. I had tried these activities a few times but soon decided that they were boring and not for me: they were for posh people. I ruled them out for myself. In my late thirties I moved into a Buddhist community in London with thirteen others. There I was mixing with people from all walks of life, and some would invite me to accompany them to various cultural events. I remembered that when I had visited an art gallery previously, I would try to look at everything. I would become thoroughly exhausted, and wonder what others got out of such a place.

A friend explained that it was best to look at just two or three paintings or sculptures which particularly attracted me, and to spend time in front of them, seeing what happened, feeling what happened, just trying to be open to the experience of looking. Is anything being communicated? Does this picture move me? He also said it would help to read a little about the artist's life. I discovered I just needed some guidance, a good teacher.

Because of this friend, I learnt that if I want to do something new, I need a teacher who knows at least a little more than me and hopefully a lot more. Or I can google the subject. I learnt that I would get more benefit from going to an opera if I had listened to the score a couple of times before going, and read the synopsis in advance. Then I would be able to let go and be open to see where the experience transported me.

So I have learnt to embrace change, and now I even welcome it. Change is exhilarating. There is hardly any excitement or experience of anything new in life without going through those familiar, fearful thoughts. That's just how it is. The alternative is to live an anxious, fear-ridden life, which will create 'dis-ease' within. By facing the fear and doing it anyway, life does get a whole lot better. Yes, not everything is enjoyable, but by taking a risk and trying something out, you can experience freedom. You can even become an example for others, encouraging them to break out into a new way of seeing and experiencing our amazing world.

'I can't change.' Yes, you can! You can't *not* change. The question is, how do you want to change?

7

What we dwell on
we become

Let me ask you this question: do you think that watching the television or tablet news – with all its horrors, vivid pictures, and scare-mongering stories – do you think that makes you happier? I haven't watched the so-called news for over twenty years now, and I know I am a happier person, who is less fearful of the world, and more content within. The broadcast news contains only the minority of life's happenings. By far the majority of life's events concern ordinary people, who are doing ordinary, positive, and helpful things for themselves and others.

Why do so many human beings choose to be saturated each day, via radio and television, or by newspapers, phones, and tablets, with so much tragedy and horror? I really don't know, but we are definitely choosing to. If we didn't watch and listen or read in our millions then the news-mongering would stop. The daily news cycle creates a strong impression that the world is a horrible place. In fact, while there are indeed great difficulties in the world, those are only a small fraction of life's events.

Although I have happily chosen not to engage directly with the news for many years, I do hear what I need to. Things are mentioned by friends, or clients, or family, but that's different from watching all those vivid images of death and horror which daily flash onto screens. Which send the message that the world is not a safe place to inhabit.

Ask yourself:

What do I dwell on?
Is it enhancing my life's happiness?
What do I do in my spare time?
Who do I mix with?
Are these people helping me to become the best I can be?
What images am I watching?

Do you play war games or killing games on the computer? I invite you to check in with your heart and listen. Is your heart becoming more loving and more connected to others? Or is it becoming more closed off and frightened? What we dwell on will make all the difference to our lives. Be sure to notice that it's you yourself doing the choosing; there is no one to blame. You are running your life.

Or are you? I encourage you to take hold of the reins of your life and reflect on what you dwell on. Consider, why *do* I dwell on the news, or on whatever it may be that doesn't lift up my world or my heart? Life is certainly short, even if we make it to ninety years old. It whizzes by. If you are young and haven't learnt that yet, just ask any older person, 'Is your life going by quickly?'

So don't wait. Often people say they don't have the time to look at their life like this. If so, I suggest that you have missed the whole point of your existence, which is very sad. You are probably just existing, just surviving, just biding time. Yet there is more to life than that. You are worth so much more than just getting by and existing.

Stop, look, feel, and listen to your deeper voices:

What is this precious life of mine for?
What do I need to dwell on, in order to create a more
    joyful, content, and happy life?

Don't delay: you can really never know if today will be your last day, can you? Make every minute, hour, and day of your life count.

If you dwell on negative thoughts and stories, hold grudges with family, friends, neighbours, or work colleagues, then let them go. It might not seem so, but freedom can be as easy as that. When you wake up to the awareness that dwelling on such negativity and holding on to past pains is creating pain for you right now, *then* things can change. You are perpetuating the pain, not the other person who it seems to be about; I doubt very much that they are suffering at this moment about this particular issue. Therefore, I encourage you to let go of all those painful stories and grudges and be kind to yourself. Love yourself.

Notice your thoughts and the effect they have on you. Notice the knock-on effect on others, which is then returned to you. How we are in this world is always mirrored back to us by other people. If we behave in an angry and negative way, others will sense such a mood and probably try to avoid us, whereas if we come across as positive, happy, and cheerful, people are drawn to us. We pick up on others' moods. If someone walks into our place of work in an angry state, we can feel it without them having to say a word. If someone is in a light, happy, and positive mood, notice how that feels very different. Then ask yourself, 'Which person am I drawn to?'

By dwelling on beauty, such as nature or uplifting music; by mixing with people who draw the best out of you, who inspire and support you to be the very best you can, there will be a deep resonance within your heart which will lift your whole being, and benefit your whole way of existence. Take the time to stop and look, to feel and listen to your own inner depths. Just sit quietly and allow yourself to be.

The world within us knows what is most helpful to our being, but we keep choosing to distract ourselves from ourselves. Then one day we will wake up old and realize how many millions of opportunities we have missed. So, however old you are now, just get started. Let your mind dwell on someone or something or somewhere that is life-enhancing, and which truly nourishes your heart and spirit.

And ask yourself, 'Now, how does *this* feel?'

8

We get in our own way

It's very common for us to look for someone to blame for any sort of suffering we are subject to. We might blame the local city council for having failed to mend a paving slab that was sticking up, one that we tripped over. But who was walking? Who was not looking where they were going? The world, as we fully know, is not perfect. Paving slabs do stick up here and there.

I have found that my life is much happier, and my stress is greatly reduced, when I take full responsibility for my life, for my actions, words, and thoughts. And when I don't blame anyone by becoming resentful, angry, or self-righteous. This doesn't mean that I won't write to the city council to ask that the paving slab be mended. It just means I can avoid the suffering of self-created negativity. The truth is, the slab was sticking up. I tripped because I was not paying attention to the path where I was walking. By writing to the council about it, I can do something to help avoid the likelihood of someone else tripping on the same paving slab. Positive actions are created like this. Then there is no need for me to go around telling people how dreadful the council is and getting more and more wound up as I tell this story more and more.

To give a more serious and far-reaching example, when I was fifteen my Mum left the family home. She was the heart and soul of the home. Two years later my Dad told me to leave, because his new wife did not want to look after his children. I had done nothing wrong, yet my life was turned upside down. I have to admit to being fully in blame, anger, and resentment mode for some years following that experience.

Some years later again, after some counselling sessions, I suddenly woke up! I saw clearly how all along it was me who was perpetuating my own suffering. I was holding on to the pain of events that had happened years earlier, and which was still ruining my life. Yes, it would have been much better for me if my Mum had not left, and my Dad had not thrown me out. The truth is Mum did leave, and Dad did throw me out. I just seemed to be in the way of their new lives.

There is, of course, the pain and suffering which is appropriate when traumatic things happen. However, in my case it was me who, for years, continued running over the same resentful and angry stories in my mind, without being able to let go of them, or forgive the people involved. Through counselling and personal growth work, I came to see that I had in fact *chosen* to be a victim. I had not been able to take full responsibility for my mental states in relation to this particular situation. When I saw what I was holding on to and realized I could let it go, I experienced such a huge relief. I could see how all along I had been getting in my own way – and how, in order to be happy, I would need to get out of it my own way.

Things happen in our lives that we don't want, and unfortunately they have a habit of continuing to happen. What we do with our mind regarding difficult events in our lives will create a pleasurable or an embittered life. These two lives are very different: we can choose either one. The choice is ours, but we don't often see clearly the reality of the situation.

Stop
Look
Feel
Listen

While on holiday last Christmas I met a lovely couple. Over a meal, one of them opened up to me about her pain concerning her best friend of fifty years: they had had a falling out. This woman was upset about what her friend had said and done; she was blaming her old friend for her own pain. We were sharing dinner on a cruise ship in the Caribbean, on a holiday of a lifetime, and my fellow passenger had chosen to bring along this pain which was so strong that I felt it tangibly. In the midst of what could have been a most joyous time, she was choosing to keep feeding a grudge from the past.

Pain certainly arises when difficult things happen between individuals, but we don't need to hold on to it: we can forgive and move on. At times, we all do things that other people don't like. Generally, we don't intend to upset someone, but that's just how life is, particularly where other people are concerned, because we are all different. We all *see* differently. Yet when we choose to perpetuate the problem by continually ruminating over it we create so much hurt for ourselves. The good news is that there is a way out of this impasse. We can try to heal the rift and dress the wound by being generous. We can be the first to speak, or send a card, for instance. One thing is certain: *both* people will be hurting, and life is too short for that to benefit anyone.

How many of us do this kind of blaming someone, or some event, or some past relationship, when things don't go the way we wish? A neighbour parks their car in front of our house, and we say, 'How dare they!' In this way we create 'dis-ease' for ourselves. Instead, we could choose to be generous to our neighbour, who is really just like us at heart. They, too, want to love and be loved. and also need to park their car somewhere. By being generous we could enjoy whatever we are doing, without getting into a stew about something that in the scale of things doesn't matter one jot.

Only this week I watched a neighbour become extremely anxious, because she wanted to go to the supermarket without losing the parking space outside her house. She decided to stay home rather than go shopping, even though there is plenty of parking around where we live. We do so limit our lives by our thoughts! Probably we have come across thousands of similar situations during our life, some big, some small, some in-between. I hope you are recognizing how we are almost programmed to get in our own way. And getting in our own way prevents the experience of freedom, ease, happiness, and contentment. It all depends on what we choose to dwell on.

There is actually no one to blame for anything; there are just circumstances. This certainly doesn't mean that when people do nasty things, they should not be brought to justice. It merely means that we don't need to continue agonizing for years over past wrongs and injustices, ruining our lives in the process, and often the lives of others close to us, too. I know that this area is very difficult to understand, and hard to agree with, initially. We have to stop, look, feel, and listen to the truth, to reality, and to our mind and what it's dwelling on.

There is a Buddhist teaching known as the Two Darts. A painful event happens. That's the first dart. The painful event hurts, and in an attempt to avoid the pain, our mind immediately clicks in with a story. That's the second dart. The first dart is momentary – the event has happened – but the second dart can remain with us sometimes for a lifetime, if we are not aware and careful. Unpleasant events in our lives are bound to happen from time to time; some will be our own fault, some not. Still, once the event has already happened we can choose whether we get in our own way or not. The first dart we can't normally prevent, but the second dart we most definitely can.

Bigger pains take time, such as the situation with my Mum and Dad. It took me years to come to terms with that, because I was not aware of what I was doing to myself. I didn't think I had a choice. I had not yet woken up to the realization that I choose my own thoughts and can therefore change them.

With the help of counselling and meditation, I began to see a different perspective. My parents did the best they knew how to. When I calmly thought about them as people like me, and saw their lives from *their* perspective, I could understand. I knew *their* parents, my grandparents, and knowing something of my grandparents' childhoods helped me to understand enormously. My great-grandmother died when my Grandma was just eleven years old, so she had had no mother figure to look to. And in 1939 my Grandma had had my Mum sent away at the age of six because of the Second World War. They didn't see one another for twenty years, until Mum was twenty-six and pregnant with me: my Mum had not had a mother figure either. Although she doted on us three children, obviously her own history gave her the permission to be able to leave us.

There will always be much more to each story than we realize at the time or could ever fully be aware of. Knowing this, we can develop compassion for all people, who, after all, are in the same human predicament as we are. And we can make our lives freer right now, better for ourselves and others, by not choosing to get in our own way.

Getting out of my own way has enhanced my life.

9

The human condition, lost in thought

We miss much of our lives, lost in thought of the past and future. I have said earlier in this book that it's never not now. Yet we cover now with a web of stories and views, and mostly we don't stop, look, and check to see if the stories are true, or whether the views are ours or up to date.

To live a life at full bloom you need to know your mind, because mind leads everything. You have a thought, then you feel an emotion in relation to the thought, then you act. And all actions have consequences in the world and on you. So the action that manifests depends on the original thought that your mind produces. Of course, just having a thought doesn't mean you then act. You can take a space to decide what effect that action, word, or deed would have in the world, because all actions have consequences, and non-actions have consequences, too.

Every word that comes out of your mouth, or that you write or type, comes from a thought, and has a consequence for you and others. In my life I have said a few things that I wish I had thought a little more about before speaking or pressing the 'send' button. I then learnt the consequences, whether helpful or not. The world normally reflects us back quite quickly. Also, if we listen to our inner world, that tells us when we have acted in a way that is unkind, untruthful, or mean. It weighs on our mind, we feel 'dis-ease' within. If we get to know our mind, listen for clarity, take space before following through on our thoughts, life will be easier.

So often we live life at such a fast pace, lost in thought – or without thinking, just reacting. Then we have to spend time sorting out any disagreement or mess we have created. By taking a moment of time *after* the thought and *before* acting, we will save time, and therefore create an easier, more pain-free life. Time is an illusion anyway: as long as we are alive, there is always time. It's just how we decide to spend the time, how we choose to spend it, and it is always us doing the choosing. If you have commitments, you decided to commit, and this means you can decide to change those commitments. That's why getting to know your mind and not being lost in thought is the only way forward if you are to live your life, the life you are here for.

To know your mind, you must take space, spend time with yourself, get to know who you are now. You can do this by walking the dog on your own in nature, sitting on the beach, walking in the woods, meditating, or by being alone in your room with electronic devices turned off. Taking such time to be with you is invaluable, and you are worth it. In the quiet, initially we hear the static of our mind: your mind won't be quiet, you are getting to know your mind, seeing what goes on within you, noticing what thoughts you are choosing. Do you want to continue such thoughts? Or would you like to dwell on something more edifying, positive, loving, or kind?

Don't take all your thoughts that seriously, there will be another lot along shortly. We can't even remember what we were anxious about last week: most thoughts don't matter as much as we make them matter. We can just be aware of them and let them flow on like clouds in the sky. The only thoughts we can deal with are the ones we are having now, and if we stop, look, feel, and listen now, we start to know who we are now. When we know the raw material of our mind, we can make wiser choices. Most of our choices tend to be habitual, from past ways of responding, which can be out of date for your life now. If the thoughts are helpful, then great, but often when we stop, look, feel, and listen to ourselves, we wake up to the ways in which we trip ourselves up. Then, when we are aware of our patterns and habits, we can change them.

I had a habit of eating a sugar-filled flapjack in the mid-afternoon. At the time I thought this was a treat when my energy was low. I had been eating this snack at work for a couple of years. I then asked myself, 'Do I feel better after the flapjack?' And realized that I didn't, sometimes it even gave me a headache, it certainly didn't help my energy. So actually what I had described to myself as a treat was not a treat. I learnt that the treat was *not* to have a sugar-filled flapjack. Instead I would snack on a punnet of raspberries or some mango: both I find delicious, and I felt better, not worse.

I have now done this stopping, looking, feeling, and listening with pretty much everything and everyone in my life. I am very grateful to all my various teachers who have shared with me so much of their wisdom. All that I share with you in these pages is because of them. Teachers come in different guises: they can be other people; they can be our mistakes and our successes.

We act from our mind and views. I recommend looking at your mind, your habits, and your views. Ask questions to really see how they affect your world. With views you may have had for years, check that they are your views, not someone else's; not those of parents, friends, or a particular culture.

What do you think now?
What do you believe?
Check your views are up to date: are they your
    views now?

Views underpin everything. Stop, look, feel, and listen, don't be lost in thought.

10

Mindfulness – be here now

The best way I have found to stop, look, feel, and listen, is to practise mindfulness. Mindfulness is synonymous with awareness, and awareness is the most effective means for knowing ourselves, our emotions, and our mind. Therefore, mindfulness can transform our lives in a way that gives most meaning, contentment, and joy, for our own future and that of other people around us.

Mindfulness is for everyone, from every walk of life. We are practising mindfulness if we are praying, meditating, reflecting – or just being present in nature, or to whatever we are doing. Be here now:

Stop, to take stock.
Look, to really see, see within, see reality.
Feel whether your body is at ease.
Listen to your deeper voices, hear messages from
  the universe.

Mindfulness, awareness, enables us to see things as they really are, and therefore to make wiser choices. If we don't stop and take stock, we are choosing to be dragged through our life by distractions, one after the other. And if we are continually distracted by distractions, then the only things that can tend to stop us in our tracks are illnesses, accidents, and deaths, which shock us into becoming awake. We then realize that our self-created tension, pain, and over-rushed lives can only create 'dis-ease' and confused choices. So how to counteract this state of affairs?

Around 500 in India the Buddha taught a meditation practice called the Mindfulness of Breathing. This practice has been transforming lives for over twenty-five centuries. It can transform yours, too – if you practise it regularly. Remember, what you dwell on, you become. Also, don't get in your own way!

Here is an outline of the Mindfulness of Breathing practice. Please also see my website (www.danapriya.org) for a free, thirty-minute audio recording of the practice led by me. It's a very simple practice: there are four stages. For the meditation to be most effective, I feel there also needs to be a stage of preparation, and a stage of completion.

To *prepare*, really become present – in your body, and emotions, and calming your mind. Scan your whole body for tensions and then release them. Let go of any worldly distractions, practise just sitting there in the midst of your precious life, with nothing to do and nowhere to go – 'Ahhhhh …'. (Spend about three minutes on this stage.)

We are now more prepared for the Mindfulness of Breathing meditation practice.

In the *first stage*, we begin by noticing our breathing. We place our awareness on the rise and fall of our tummy as the breath comes and goes in its own rhythm. We are not doing the breathing, we have been breathing since we were born, our body knows what to do. We are just placing awareness on the breath, watching it come and go. We then add a silent count at the end of the out-breath. So we breathe in and breathe out, count 'one', breathe in and breathe out, count 'two', and so on, up to ten. We then go back to count 'one' again.

We may get to the number three and our mind wanders off somewhere, this is absolutely fine, that's what minds do. When we realize we are not meditating but thinking, we can then return with kindness to our breath and start at 'one' again. Our mind may wander off many times in a practice, yet that is not a problem, we just keep kindly returning to being present to our breathing life force. (Spend about four minutes on this stage.)

In the *second stage* we move the count to the beginning of the in-breath. Count 'one', breathe in, breathe out, count 'two', breathe in, breathe out, and so on, up to ten. Before the next in-breath begins, we then go back to count 'one' again. (Spend about four minutes on this stage.)

In the *third stage* we let go of the count, and just watch our body breathe. Maybe our tummy rises and falls, our chest moves, maybe we feel our back and sides moving, we are just being interested in the amazing, subtle rhythm. We don't do anything but be aware and notice. Yet our wonderful mind will wander off again and again. When we realize this, we just return with kindness to watching our precious body breathe. (Spend about four minutes on this stage.)

In the *fourth stage* we place all our awareness and focus on the part of the body where we feel the air coming into our body. This is usually the upper lip, nostrils, and maybe in the mouth and the back of the throat. The air is coming in and is going out of our body, we are just being interested, and seeing if we can feel the sensations while the rest of our body is totally relaxed. (Spend about four minutes on this stage.)

To *complete* the practice, let go of watching your breath. Just sit doing absolutely nothing, absorbing the results of your efforts. (Spend about three minutes on this stage).

That's the Mindfulness of Breathing meditation. This practice is about being here in our fullness, wholly attending; about gathering all of our disparate pieces in one place, at one time, so our mind and body are together, and present to what is happening, now. We then receive clearly from our senses, and our environment. This brings a greater clarity, and a richness of experience that is normally numbed by distraction and our inattentiveness.

People who do this practice talk about being grounded, or centred, or that they feel 'together' and 'collected'. They then feel like they are plugged into what is best in themselves, and to what is utmost in the universe. If we practise the Mindfulness of Breathing regularly, we will feel like our lives are in a flow, going in a direction that feels easy and right, and we will more likely be doing what we were meant to be doing in this lifetime.

So many people miss most of their lives through unawareness. Don't be someone who one day wakes up old, and wonders where their life went. Be here now. It's never not now. Try the practice today by listening to the free Mindfulness of Breathing audio recording at www.danapriya.org.

11

Grief and love

Grief is a part of life. Grief is healthy; as one of our core emotions, it needs to live. Yet so often we can be embarrassed to cry, and we feel weak when we express our sadness. Actually, to cry with others is strong, and to talk with people about our loss is healthy. We did love those people and all those things we have lost, and it's totally appropriate to grieve. After all, we grieve to the degree that we have loved. How would a life be if we did not love?

All your emotions need to flow in order for you to be fully alive and at ease. Not allowing yourself to cry at the cinema or at a funeral, and trying to keep a stiff upper lip, is a tragedy for your soul and your heart. We are born to emote, in fact we are e-motion; for a human being to be at ease, to be free from 'dis-ease', emotional energy needs to live, mentally, physically, *and* emotionally.

How we are, how we let ourselves be, is wholly our responsibility. What's more, our example can help others, too. If you see someone being loving, it will warm your heart and encourage you to be more loving. If you are with someone who is crying, that may give you permission to cry with them.

In this way you can be the one to encourage others, to give them permission to flow with life.

How do you feel when you have allowed yourself to grieve, to cry? 'Relieved' is what most people say, 'That's better.' Crying is a letting go of what we have lost, a letting go of what we are holding on to, a letting go of how we think we should act in society for fear of being seen as weak. For most people it takes great courage to let go in public, even when we feel secure with family and friends. Courage is not weak, but brave and healthy. Your body, heart, and soul will feel so much better if you can let go. I hope this insight will resonate with you at a deep level. When we stop, look, feel and listen, we will spontaneously know how we feel, and then our emotions will be able to flow.

So often we do not actually feel; we are just not in touch with our experience in the present moment. We wear a mask for the occasion, a mask that our mind, not our emotions, is telling us to wear amongst these particular people. At different times we will wear different masks: one mask for when we are at home, one for work, one for the gym, and one with friends, or when we go on holiday. We have many faces and many behaviours, which we display in different situations. Which one we adopt will depend on how we think we ought to be, or what we think will make us acceptable and lovable to this particular group of people – whereas we could just flow with life, being authentic to our unfolding self.

Of course, I realize that there are many situations in which it would not be sensible to express raw emotion. Suppose, say, you are frustrated with a member of your family: to let out a tirade of anger at them won't be forgotten in a day or two. It won't foster love, it will just create more grief. But the raw emotion of that frustration does need to live and needs to be expressed. Learning how to do this skilfully will help both you and the member of your family, as well as everyone else involved.

You may, for instance, choose to say nothing at the time, deciding to talk about it later with a friend, one who is not emotionally involved. In that way you may gain a new perspective on the situation. Then, at a later date and with a broader view, you may be able to talk calmly with the member of your family, in a way that they can hear exactly what you are finding so difficult. Together you may be able to help one another resolve any difficulties, rather than setting up a battle or continuing a fight. Another strategy is to go for a run or a brisk walk, which can channel the pent-up energy in a positive direction. In Chapter 12 I discuss the effects of words and communication. It's not pleasant for anyone if we create a stink, and generally such behaviour harms all concerned. However, the energy of the emotion does need to live.

Wearing so many masks is exhausting. Being a different person to so many different people is anxiety-provoking, stressful, and disintegrating. One of the main purposes of any personal growth work is to integrate ourselves into one person – one person who is going in one direction, and who is confident and proud of their true self. To be truly able to love other people, it is vital to be the person we deeply are, and to love that person: this is the subject of Chapter 16. Living a life in full bloom means that all our emotions will be alive, flowing fully and lovingly for ourselves and others.

We need to learn how *not* to hold our emotions in. Suppressing them will create tension, rigidity, and stiffness, and affect us adversely – mentally and physically, as well as emotionally. When we don't express our emotions, we tend to think that no one else can see them, because we are not showing them externally. Yet our body language gives it all away. Our hidden emotions will be very clearly felt by others, and particularly by those who know us well.

To take a common example: you work with someone day in, day out, and one morning they come in and that usual spark is not there. They have a forlorn look, and immediately you feel the difference between how they normally are, and how they are now. You sense something is wrong, even without any words being exchanged. You enquire, 'How are you?' And they reply, 'Oh, I'm fine, thanks.' You know they are not telling the whole story. Their answer is not congruent with their body language, or with who you know them to be.

This is a kind of emotional lying. Lying has never helped anyone because it breeds distrust of what a person says. If you can't trust a person's words, this will cause a lot of grief. But often people do not realize they are lying; they may not be sufficiently aware of their feelings to be able to be honest. Or maybe they have too much fear to allow themselves to be vulnerable, and in an attempt to protect themselves they put the barriers up. This fools no one and helps no one.

I am sure you will have had many similar experiences of things not quite adding up when communicating with others. All you can do is to be authentic yourself. Stop, look, feel, and listen. Know yourself, integrate yourself. You will be able to help others best when you are emotionally, mentally, and physically honest; when you are *one being* going in *one direction*, a being who is loving, and who grieves easily. Integration and honesty, like loving and grieving, go together. Things arise, things fall; people are born, people die. This is the beautiful dance we are all part of.

Do you want to sit like a wallflower throughout your life?
Or do you want to be someone who can glide around the
dance floor of life with a heart in full bloom?

Do remember, however, that the extent to which we grieve is equal to the depth of our love, and a life without love would be tragic.

12

Talk that perfumes the air

As an ordained Buddhist, I have undertaken training in observing ten principles or ideals which help and guide me to live a happier, more human life. Of these ten ideals, four focus on speech. So just under half of my training principles are about words, speech, and communication.

Sometimes, it seems, we can choose to create a right mess with other people, a mess strewn with misunderstandings, unkindnesses, insensitivity, hastiness, untimeliness, and downright lying, or else with ways of communicating that we have just not thought through. Yet in other situations, we can choose to leave a beautiful perfume in our wake, moving around the planet and touching all those with whom we have contact in a way that is timely, helpful, kindly, clear, honest, and generous.

Speech can be so automatic, words can easily be spoken without much thought. It's at this point that we need to stop or at least slow down a little. We need to create a gap between the thought of what we want to say, and the actual saying of it. Pausing to check the thought, before speaking, is the best way to communicate what we wish to convey. Then not only the words, but also the spirit of the communication will be effective and beneficial.

Here is a useful set of questions to use when checking a thought before speaking:

Does it need saying at all?
Is it a good time to say it?
Is it helpful?
Is it kind?
Is it creating harmony?
Is it true?
Does it create connection?

When you can answer 'Yes' to all of these, then you will have a good chance of being a much more effective and beautiful communicator. You will be choosing to create for others, and for yourself, an easier life containing much more love. It's really not complicated.

In my experience, texting and social media services such as WhatsApp are among the worst culprits for tripping us up, and for creating disharmony and misunderstanding. The messaging happens so quickly. You hastily tap out a few words and press 'send' without further ado. But those few words can be read in many different ways, and the recipient can understand your message differently from the way you intended. This can be a surefire way to create discord.

A reply will come flying back with the same ill-thought-through speed, which in turn will create upset for you. You wonder where that particular response came from, or how the sender could react in such a way. Have you ever been in this situation? It's not very helpful for anyone, and it certainly doesn't leave a beautiful fragrance in its wake, only a mess to be cleared up. Emails can be just as bad. Having received an email we decide we don't like, we bang out a quick retort, and press the 'send' button extra hard, while saying to ourselves something like, 'Take that!' Is this the best we can do?

I try to follow the rule that, if there is an important communication to be exchanged, which has to be done via email, I write my response but don't send it immediately. I will read it again the next day, change it if necessary, and only then will I press the 'send' button. By calmly delaying in this way I have found that I am much more likely to receive a pleasant and appreciative reply: people respond to kindness, honesty, and clarity.

Every communication can be a delight to send and receive. This contributes to life being more heartening for ourselves and others. We are also, incidentally, more likely to get what we need. So ask yourself:

What outcome would I like with my communication?
What is the best way to get that outcome?

When a cold-caller telephones while you are in the middle of cooking dinner, remember that they, too, are a person, like you. They certainly want to be loved and to love; they, too, have pleasures and pains, and need to earn a living. When speaking with them, you can just say a kind, 'No, thank you.'

Not long ago I received an email from a friend, his response of 'No' to a request I had made. It was the nicest 'No' I have ever received. I saved that email and still refer to it when I want to say 'No'. This is what he wrote: 'Hi there, my dear! How kind of you to think of me! I am afraid I'm going to have to say no. (I'm trying to learn this art!) I'm not around on those days of the event. Always lovely to see you. Much love.'

Recently I have started doing something which is delightfully old-fashioned: I am writing letters to people. When I write by hand I find I consider my words more, and I notice the spirit they are creating between the reader and me. I have time to reflect on what I have written, because of the time it takes to write the letter or the card, as well as the time taken to address the envelope, stick on the stamp, and walk to the postbox. There is something lovely about putting a letter to a friend into the postbox, and imagining them receiving it, hopefully enjoying the surprise.

Indeed, for me there is a big difference between opening my email inbox, and a letter falling onto my doormat. When opening a letter or a card, I find myself savouring the words and the experience; whereas opening my email inbox – with its many emails (most of which I delete) – and seeing the email from my friend will only provide a limited sort of pleasure. I wonder if you have ever had that experience?

In this chapter so far I have written about various forms of communication without mentioning speaking! As we well know, to stop and think, even for a couple of seconds, or the length of one breath, before talking or responding, can make the difference between creating a beautiful perfume or a stink. There *is* enough time in the day. So often we can feel pressed for time; it's as though our whole way of life is being lived as one big rush to the crematorium.

Stop, breathe, 'take the time to smell the roses', and you will find you are being more effective. You will get more done in a relaxed and graceful way, and anxiety will lessen. Remember, it's you who is choosing to live in a state of hurry and angst, or you are choosing to live calmly and effectively. Your choice will create two very different worlds, and it's up to you which one you inhabit. Speaking with awareness can be learnt; you do have time to choose how you use your words.

When I started to reflect on how I affect the world through my speech I had a rather shocking realization about how much I lied. I became aware that I had a long-term habit of either exaggerating or understating things – depending on which I thought would make me look better in the opinion of the hearer. Of course, this was all projected thinking, because I couldn't really know what the other person thought, unless I asked them.

We try to please someone by saying what we think they want to hear. We don't ask, we guess and then we speak. This happens within the blink of an eye and can go terribly wrong because we have guessed incorrectly. We then realize that what we said was not the truth anyway; that, if only we had told the truth in the first place, the communication would have been a whole lot easier. Also, when we lie, we immediately fear being found out. We think that, if we are discovered, that person won't easily trust us again, which may well be true.

Lies can be of the very small, so-called 'white' variety, but they are lies just the same. Seventy-two people attended my forty-ninth birthday party, and it was wonderful to see all those people. While I was shopping the next day, someone said to me, 'Hi, Danapriya! How was your birthday party? I'm sorry I couldn't make it.' 'It was wonderful,' I replied, 'there were over a hundred people there.' Seventy-two people is pretty impressive, but it's not one hundred. I exaggerated, and this is basically a form of lying. The tendency to exaggerate is usually connected with issues around self-worth. If I feel a poverty within, then externally I will try to make things look better than they are, whereas if I feel abundant and integrated within, I will not need to make things up to feel better. I will know that I'm all right as I am.

Stop, breathe, think, and then tell the truth without exaggeration or understatement. It's always possible to choose speech that is kind, and we can always choose to communicate in a friendly way. It's fine, indeed natural, that we won't like every person we come into contact with, but we can, at least, treat everyone with respect. For a compassionate world, it's desirable to treat everyone as we would like to be treated ourselves, to speak to everyone in the way we would wish to be spoken to.

This practice with words, speech, and communication is so simple.

If we can communicate with honesty, in a kindly, meaningful, and harmonious fashion, then usually there will be a good outcome for ourselves, the other person, and the world as well. We will always feel better after a heartening conversation, an honest conversation, a meaningful conversation. Everyone wins. If you can do this, then you will leave a beautiful and impressive perfume in your wake, wherever you go.

13

Have courage and be kind

The title of this chapter is taken from a film I watched recently: the 2015 Disney version of Cinderella, with Lily James playing the title role. About ten minutes into the film, Cinderella's mother is about to die. She invites her daughter into her room for the last time, and says to her, 'Ella ... you must always remember this: have courage and be kind.... It has power, more than you know, and magic, truly.' The advice makes for an incredible moment.

The film then shows how Cinderella continually finds courage and kindness, in the face of an absolutely dreadful childhood and early adulthood. Although her father dies, her stepsisters are evil, and her stepmother is even worse, in the simplicity of her courage and kindness, Cinderella glides on to have an amazing life. This phrase, 'Have courage and be kind,' has stayed with me. If I can continually apply these qualities to my life, I believe life will have a power and magic beyond my imagination.

With courage in your toolbox, you can keep changing and growing when things are not going well. You can also try out something new. Courage works against all those irrational fears that we so often don't know are limiting us. Together with kindness to ourselves and others, courage creates strength and beauty.

This is a short chapter – I believe there is power in simplicity. And what if, 'Have courage and be kind' can be a complete life philosophy?

14

Heroes and heroines

If we are to evolve, develop, and learn, we need heroes and heroines to inspire us: teachers and mentors to look up to, or even friends to emulate, who are just a little further along the path of personal growth. Such mentors or friends are examples of something more than we are at present.

Whether we like it or not, hierarchy does exist in our society, and hierarchy is essential for us to be able to learn. Natural hierarchy is not based on power over people, it just means that some people know more in some areas than others. We all have skills which we can share and pass on to each other. When I moved out of London, for instance, I wanted to have some singing lessons. Of course, I wanted to be taught by someone who sang better than me, someone who knew how to get the best out of people's voices.

When it came to my spiritual life and the area of personal growth, I didn't realize at first that I was looking for a teacher, a hero or a heroine. In fact, I found many teachers, all having different gifts to share. During the past thirty years I have learnt from philosophers, authors, friends, mentors, therapists, and other human beings whom I came across, and was able to share some of life's gems with.

My experience is that, when I meet someone, maybe a teacher in person, or their new perspective on life, I want to share what I learn. I naturally want to be generous and pass it on. The paradox of knowing something is that you can keep giving the knowledge away, yet still possess it. Knowledge is abundant, unlike material things which, once given away, have gone.

By heroes and heroines I mean the people you can look up to with confidence. People who help to give your life meaning, who reveal something you had not seen before, maybe even something beyond the ordinary – sometimes heroes and heroines can be slightly 'not of this world'. The heroes and heroines that the media present to us in our society seem to be limited to television stars and sportspeople. No matter how lovely these people are, this is not what I am talking about here, unless you are wanting to be a professional sportsperson, or a television star.

The people who have helped me most throughout my life have challenged my *views* about life, about how I thought about it, which has helped me to see through my own delusions. For instance, in Chapter 22 I talk about not knowing when we will die, and about that being life-enhancing rather than morbid. Having understood this, I try to make each moment count, rather than fritter my life away.

I also came to see that I can create my own suffering by what I do with my mind. I realized that I can free myself from so many of life's difficulties by just seeing differently, by understanding and accepting difference. And much more besides.

One person who has helped me greatly has done so by quietly and gently continuing to invite me, and encourage me, to be more. He saw my potential, which my inner world – with all its fears and stories – didn't allow, couldn't see. This book would not have been written without his wise words. In a Skype conversation, I told him that I felt like I needed to write a book, but this seemed like far too grand a notion for me. He said, 'Well, Danapriya, you didn't think you could start a Buddhist Group, did you?' 'Ah,' I thought, 'you've got me there,' because I had set up and run a very successful Buddhist Group for eleven years, which is still thriving. This gave me the spur to begin writing, and quite quickly twenty-five chapters came onto the page.

There is a well-known Buddhist text, the Dhammapada, or 'Way of Truth', which starts with two verses about recognizing that all experience is produced by the mind. So, to be happy, I need to take full responsibility for what my mind is doing. And to get to know my mind, I need to practise stopping, looking, feeling, and listening. I need to reflect and meditate. I need to take time walking in nature, or time just to be alone. This is what will help me carry on evolving, learning, and growing, and developing an open mind and heart.

So it's worth asking:

Who are my heroes and heroines?
And why?

15

Giving creates love

When we think about giving, charities often come to mind first. We think about the giving of money, the coins in a collection box, the standing orders made out to causes that are valuable to us, or giving some cash to homeless people. This way of being generous is certainly needed. It makes such a difference in our world and helps us feel connected to other people and the environment.

Yet there are so many other ways that we can choose to give, ways that will create love and fill the atmosphere with kindness. They are often small things, such as a smile. I make a habit of regularly smiling to a stranger, and, nine times out of ten, the other person responds with a smile. A magic fills the air between us; it connects us in a very simple, human way; the smile brightens my day and, I believe, the other person's world, too. Such small acts of generosity go beyond judgement, beyond like and dislike, beyond boundaries. What's more, they are easy and don't cost anything.

Little things go a long way. Have courage and be kind. Giving a warm welcome to anyone we are greeting, being pleased to see them, taking their coat, offering them a seat, all these small acts make a difference. We can smile and shake hands, or hug if appropriate; a receptive body language and a generous spirit always have a positive effect on the world and on us. Placing a hand on someone's shoulder at an appropriate moment when, for instance, they may have just received some bad news, can go a long way. Showing support in this simple fashion can feel very helpful for the receiver.

The possibilities for kindness are endless. Opening a door for someone. Giving up a seat on a train or bus for a person who may need it more. Paying a compliment, which may fill someone's heart and lift their mood. Offering a flower from your garden. Even thinking with kindness and care about someone is far more powerful than we generally believe. Sending love, healing, and kindness over the airwaves will help us, and I am convinced it will benefit the other person as well. So I encourage you to give something every day. These precious things are easily possible without money; they are free.

Many other positive actions, words, and qualities can be given, too: listening, for instance, and energy, courage, encouragement, time, patience, friendship, humour, empathy, kindly speech, touch, practical help, education, our example, silence, company, a meal, rejoicing, interest, and material things that are needed, to name but a few. I could probably write a chapter on each one of these ways of giving, and how they all create love. Maybe I will one day, but for now I hope you can see how *free* and *simple* the act of giving can be. This generous way of being connects us with each other, it creates meaning and love.

Here are some other examples of giving: caring for a friend, family member, or neighbour when they are unwell or in need. Speaking well of people in their absence. Doing things the way other people like them done. Ringing people up and sending cards, even writing letters – old-fashioned, maybe, but a real gift to receive. Sharing ideas and arousing energy to fundraise for meaningful causes. In short, the giving of ourselves. Altruism and generosity make a huge difference in our world.

I hope you are seeing that giving is not about material wealth. You do not need to be rich to be generous. You can have a generous heart, a generous spirit, a generous mind feeling absolutely abundant, yet have very little on a material level. Or you can be mean-hearted, mean-spirited, and mean-minded, yet have absolutely everything on a material level. Who is happier?

Often the person who has more in a material sense will feel they have more to lose. They have more to hold on to, which leads to more stress, more anxiety, and more fear of it being taken away. Actually, it doesn't matter *what* you have. Giving is about your inner world, your inner sense of self, and the degree to which you acknowledge and live from your inner riches and wealth. Then the act of giving, of being spontaneously generous, will help you feel abundant in heart, spirit, *and* mind.

I wish to talk a little about receiving generosity, receiving others' gifts. If no one receives, generosity is halted. Receiving can be easy or it can be complicated. We can appreciate the other person's effort, thoughtfulness, and kindness and receive a gift well, or we can react by saying something like, 'Oh, you shouldn't have,' feeling somehow indebted and uncomfortable, and decline whatever is being offered. When someone next gives you something, take a moment to stop, look, feel, and listen to whatever is happening in your inner world.

Ask yourself: do I receive easily or do I complicate things? I encourage you to try to receive everything well – this feeds the flow of generosity. If you are given a gift you don't need, you can receive it with thanks, and pass it on to someone who does need it. It's yours to do with whatever you like. To give it to someone else doubles the generosity.

I have a box of unwanted gifts, which I dip into when the moment arises, to be able to give appropriately to someone when they need something. Recently I was given two copies of an interesting book; I already own a copy of this book, but I welcomed the gifts, knowing that I would easily be able to find someone to pass them on to, someone who would appreciate them. When receiving the gifts, I didn't need to mention that I already have this book: doing so wouldn't help the giver feel happy about the gift they chose for me, especially because it was an ideal gift. The box of gifts to re-gift keeps my energy of giving flowing. It's also ecologically effective and has the advantage that my cupboards don't fill with unwanted stuff!

Sharing is an important subject when discussing generosity. A mind that is able to share is a generous mind. A mind that can share breaks down the separation between people, it opens up hearts and connects us to each other. A mind that's able to share works against any tendency towards greed, hatred, or delusion. These are the direct opposite of generosity, which keep us limited and produce painful states of mind.

If I find myself, for instance, harbouring ill will towards someone, then by reaching out and sharing, I experience a radical shift in my mind. When I give something or speak harmonious and kindly words, or when I send a positive thought or a card, my mind is released from pain, and I am connected to others. Whether or not they are able to receive my open-hearted kindness is, of course, not really my concern. I can't control, or even predict, their response. Yet the act of sharing will be liberating and will create an opportunity for connection and healing.

Giving is expansive and connecting. It creates friendship, good feeling, and positive emotions. Giving is pleasurable, receiving is pleasurable; seeing someone give is pleasurable, seeing someone receive is pleasurable. Giving creates a magical field of delight where positivity and love arise. It generates more giving, so why not try it?

Seeing someone being selfish is distasteful. Seeing someone being mean is grating. Seeing someone being greedy is unpleasant. Whereas generosity, in its myriad forms, perfumes the air, warms the heart, and inspires. Your examples will shine and make a difference in the world, because giving creates love.

16

Let your love live

You are absolutely stuffed full of love. Where else could it be? But you can choose whether you allow it to live. As human beings, to lead a happy and healthy life we need to receive love from others, and we also need to give love. Love is as essential as breathing, eating, and drinking. Without it we would shrivel up both emotionally and psychologically.

If I choose to give love, to share my love, to be loving and kind to others, including animals and other beings, then I will receive plenty of love. If I fear giving love, and lack courage in opening up my emotions to others, and can't risk being vulnerable, then I have closed my heart to love. Most of us have had our heart broken in some way during our life, or feel we have been ill-treated or betrayed. When these things happen we can put a padlock on our heart, the drawbridge can be raised, and the castle of our love is shut. Then we are choosing to let the person we feel harmed by close our heart, sometimes for years. We have chosen to let them win.

I tend to feel we are all so much more than that. If we could just step back and take a good, broad look at ourselves, we may then find we are able to have the courage to be kind to ourselves, and to allow the love that is stuffed inside us live and be shared – especially in the face of pain. Letting our love live is the one great way of healing, and of having the support we need.

This love which we need to *receive* and to *give* will enable us to find the courage to forgive, and help us flow on as a fully alive, loving human being on this amazingly precious journey that we call our life. Yet I have found that I need help to be able to keep my love flowing. When faced with difficulty, I really just want to close the door and let people leave me alone. When I really look at that type of reaction in myself, I begin to see that it only amounts to a small part of me: for the most part I want to connect with the people whom I love and trust, and feel supported by. Instead of connecting, I can choose to cut myself off, maybe sometimes because I feel ashamed in some way.

Our emotional world can so easily be complicated, especially by us. We can listen to the radio and empathize with people abroad who are suffering the effects of an earthquake; we can feel care, concern, and love for them, even though we have never met them. Yet we can be out of communication with our next-door neighbour, or a member of our own family, and be harbouring ill will towards them.

In every moment we have a choice. We can choose to be friendly or unfriendly, considerate or inconsiderate, generous or mean, patient or frustrated, loving or hateful, helpful or unhelpful, passionate or uncompassionate, sharing our joy or holding on to it, empathizing or not. For a happy, healthy individual life for ourselves and for all that lives in our world, it should be obvious which state of mind we need to choose. What thoughts would you rather have? Every word, action, kindness, or unkindness starts with a thought. Love and positive emotion are the answer to almost every problem the world faces today. Money won't solve the problems. Technology won't, either.

In this chapter, I am encouraging you to allow all your positive emotion to flow out from your precious life force, enhancing not only your own life, but also that of everyone you come into contact with. This is easier said than done, but it most certainly can be achieved. One tool that has greatly helped me, and millions of others, is a meditation practice called the Cultivation of Loving-Kindness. This is a simple practice which can help us contact friendliness, consideration, generosity, patience, understanding, love, helpfulness, compassion, shared joy, empathy, and kindness. It's not so much that we develop these qualities, but more that we recognize we have these qualities within us – and can allow them to flourish.

I have witnessed many individuals transform their emotional world by the Cultivation of Loving-Kindness meditation, which is also known by its original name, the Metta Bhavana. It was first taught over 2500 years ago in India and is still effective today. Here is an outline of the Cultivation of Loving-Kindness practice, in five stages. Please see my website (www.danapriya.org) for a free, thirty-minute audio recording of the practice led by me.

In the *first stage*, we focus on ourselves. We come first, because we can't be harmonious and loving on the outside if we are full of conflict or negativity on the inside. If we can experience our own self-worth and feel love towards ourselves, we will feel abundant and have lots of love to give to others. We will become more aware of the positive and warmer aspects of ourselves and will let them live and flow.

We already cherish and care for ourselves by keeping safe and looking after our health; by washing and clothing ourselves; by having friends, and maybe even going on holidays. Loving ourselves simply means liking ourselves for who we are, not comparing ourselves with others. When we have positive feelings towards ourselves, it becomes much easier to like others and not to feel threatened by them.

We just sit quietly meditating on our qualities and wishing ourselves well. We can drop in a thought, such as, 'May I be happy,' for we surely don't want to be unhappy; 'May I be well,' for we don't want to be unwell; 'May I be free from any suffering,' for we certainly don't wish to suffer. Then we just wait. We let the well-wishing messages drop like pebbles into a well, allow them to touch our depths, until little bubbles of energy spring up into life, which may produce a beautiful fountain of love, rising up and filling our being. By doing this, we are gently permitting what is already there to surface. Because of past hurts, we often choose to keep our positive emotions dormant and hidden. When we give them this opportunity, they may surge forth like a hot geyser in Iceland.

In the *second stage*, we think of a dear friend, someone we already care for and feel love towards. We remember a time when we were together, allowing ourselves to re-experience that feeling, a 'felt sense' of our connection and friendship. We are not trying to squeeze emotion out of our heart; we are just allowing what is already there to appear, if we can but stop, look, feel, and listen. Then we wish our friend well, thinking,

'May they be happy,' and 'May they be free from suffering,' and in our mind's eye seeing them joyful, hearing them laugh, feeling their support and kindness.

For the *third stage*, we choose someone whom we don't know very well, a so-called 'neutral' person. This could be someone we see regularly, such as our postperson, a neighbour, or someone at work; they are familiar but we don't know their history. In fact, they are just like us: they have their hopes and fears, their pleasures and pains, their contented times and anxious moments. We hold them in mind, wishing them happiness and good health, together with the thought, 'May they not suffer in any way.'

We are surrounded by 'neutral' people. The more we cultivate a sense of connection with them, the less we will fear the world around us, because we see these people are just like us. Who knows? If we knew them and their story we might find we really like them, even love them. It would certainly reduce all the negative projections we can transfer onto others without ever having spoken to them. Such projections only create a world of fear and tension.

In the *fourth stage*, we bring to mind someone we are having difficulty with, someone with whom we are a little upset or frustrated, and then we choose to see another side of them. They are loved, they love, deep down they certainly want to be happy and healthy, and to feel their heart sing, too.

At times we all do things that upset people, not necessarily on purpose, but just because we see things differently. It's absolutely fine to agree to differ. If we truly feel love for ourselves and others, we don't need to have everybody agree with us, or even like us. We just understand that different people have had different life histories and have therefore come to different views and ways of understanding the world. That's perfect, because if we can accept how things are, and if we don't resist the truth, then no one will suffer. We can just *enjoy* the fact of variety in our multifaceted universe.

In this stage, we reflect on the person whom we find difficult or don't agree with; we don't get involved with our story about them, which may, for instance, be full of self-righteousness. We send them well-wishing thoughts of friendliness: 'May they not create suffering for themselves,' 'May they experience joy and good health, too.' They are just like us, just like me and you, and they are much more than the limited perspective which we choose to focus on will reveal.

In the *last stage*, we imagine all four people together: ourselves, our friend, the neutral person, and the person we find challenging, allowing an equal sense of common humanity between us all – a basic, beautiful connection. We are all living on this planet just now, trying to do our best with what we have learnt so far from life. We summon up a sense of equal love for each person. Then we slowly open out our loving awareness to include friends and family, our neighbours, all the people in our towns, our country, on the planet, and out into the universe: a well-wishing to all sentient beings which allows our love to touch all of life. As explored in Chapter 3, it's worth pondering that many of these people are doing things which enable us to live rich lives.

So let your love live. My dream is that one day this practice will be taught to all schoolchildren. If this had occurred when we were very young, it could have taught us all to live a much more happy, contented, and realistic life.

For a free download of the Cultivation of Loving-Kindness meditation practice led by me, see www.danapriya.org.

17

Discipline is enjoyable

Does your soul have the space to fly, to dance and sing
   and run?
Does your spirit sit with the full moon and ponder?
Do you lie down in the long grass and look at the sky?
Do you make time for deepening your friendships?

I need the friend of discipline to enable all of these and more,
much more. People suffer because they can't live from their
deepest place. They are not in touch with their full human
potential. Many people miss much of their lives through
distraction and being scattered, living in the future or the past,
taking part in a soap opera, rather than really being here now.
We are human *beings*, not human *doings*!

Moments in nature or listening to music can certainly create
blissful experiences. Nevertheless, often we don't create the
conditions to be really present, so as to receive the blissful
moments. For more presence to arise we need to be integrated,
and to experience positive emotion – and for both we need to
make friends with discipline. This friend will free us from the
trap of missing our lives.

The key that unlocks the trap is the discipline of stopping, looking, feeling, and listening – which means creating spaces for mindful moments, and having the courage to be silent and alone. By meditating, reflecting, or merely allowing gaps for your thoughts to collect themselves, you will see more deeply, feel your emotions more deeply, and listen more clearly. Then you may see exactly what you need to do in order to live from your deeper voices, your deeper yearnings, and you will know how to let your higher aspirations come to life.

What does your heart really yearn for? Mine yearns for knowing the truth. Mine yearns for love, beauty, and ecstasy. Mine yearns for evolving, for going beyond my limited self, for going beyond my self-created struggles. The spiritual life is a life of continuing to outgrow oneself. If we are to know the truth and evolve, and to enjoy love, beauty, and ecstasy in our lives, then we need discipline as a friend. I know through experience that discipline has been kind to me. Let me tell you some ways I personally engage with this friend, discipline.

Firstly, the disciplines of *sleep*, *exercise*, and *food*: I have learnt that by getting these three aspects to work in harmony, everything in our life will go well. Often we don't give these three fundamental components of our life serious enough consideration or attention.

If we are unlucky enough to experience insomnia, it would be good to take note and do something about it. I believe pills are not the answer, since they often complicate things further by creating different problems. However, many aspects of personal growth work can help. Plenty of people say that daily meditation helps them sleep better. Also, by creating mindfulness in their lives, they start to be able to create more space in their day. They then reduce the tension in their minds and bodies, enabling them to see things differently.

Meditating on loving-kindness, for example, helps to create more positive emotion, which enhances our life no end. In an ongoing process, our communication and relationships improve, then we are likely to have less weighing on our mind, then our conscience is freer, and as a consequence we are more likely to sleep, or sleep more deeply.

Then there is the huge area of food: what you eat, when you eat, how often you eat, and in what conditions you eat. Learn to notice the effects of particular foods: do they make you feel healthier, or do you reach for foods for comfort, only to find later that you feel worse?

Do you overeat or undereat?

How exactly are you nourishing this amazing mind,
    body, and spirit of yours?

I would not be functioning well at all without having examined my food intake. This involved working out what I should eat and what I should cut out of my diet. I found that wheat, sugar, dairy products, chocolate, alcohol, hot spices, and caffeine did me no favours whatsoever, so I gladly chose to avoid them. I feel much happier and healthier now: my mind is brighter, my energy is stronger, and I sleep better. My body is more comfortable to inhabit.

Eating wisely requires the friend of discipline, the discipline to eat three meals a day without snacking in between, to eat at the same times every day, and to avoid eating late at night (as this can disturb sleep). We need to be especially vigilant when tired, as this is likely to be when we reach for 'comfort food' – which is the opposite of comfort, really, as we normally grab foods that are no good for us.

The third important discipline in life is exercise, exercising as fully as each of us can in relation to our individual ability. I was greatly encouraged by watching a YouTube video clip about the London Marathon. An eighty-nine-year-old man was interviewed about completing his twenty-third marathon; there followed an interview with an eighty-six-year-old woman who had just finished her eighteenth. Hearing them speak was inspiring and positively challenging in equal measure. I thought, 'Well, if they can do that, then I have no excuse.' I started to run.

Although my aim was to give my lungs and heart some exercise to extend my longevity, I was surprised to find how much I enjoyed running in nature and feeling the freedom of it. Over time I felt much better all round. Unless we enjoy what we do, we will not do it for very long, so each of us needs to find the exercise that works for us. This generally means going beyond our comfort zone and trying new activities. Above all, when we find what we love and find that it helps, we should invite the friend of discipline to keep us at it, come rain or shine.

I could say so much more about these areas of sleep, food, and exercise, but hopefully you can see how addressing them can bring immediate benefits to your life, and to those around you. I believe if we eat well and exercise well, we will sleep well. Then many other aspects of our life will be more enjoyable and beautiful.

Let's look briefly at a few other areas that you may like to consider concerning the beauty of discipline. There is the discipline of input. 'What we dwell on we become' is the title of Chapter 7, where I suggest you take seriously what you watch, what you read, who you mix with and what you focus on, since all create who you are becoming. By dwelling on positive aspects of society, and on gratitude, the world appears one way; whereas by dwelling on news that is highly weighted towards the negative, and not knowing which parts of the news to believe anyway, the world will look unsafe. So which world do you want to live in?

There is the discipline of not buying things. Do we really need another whatever-it-is? The sofa, for example, is still comfortable and in good order, but – be it through fashion, or boredom, or a wish for change – we may put pressure on ourselves to buy a new one. This adds to the stress of needing to earn enough money to purchase the next sofa, or we choose to live with a debt hanging over us. Picking the right sofa can also be stressful. This is just one example out of thousands, but I am sure you get the picture. Not feeling compelled to buy things gives us freedom, avoids creating financial stress, and is ecologically helpful for our universe.

Apart from my bed, which is new, my entire home is comfortably furnished with second-hand goods, most of which have been given to me by friends who are choosing to upgrade. I love my home. When I look at one sofa it brings to mind the dear friend who gave it to me, and when I look at another it brings to mind my lovely singing teacher. My dining table was given to me by old housemates, and all the pictures on the walls are gifts from friends. I love being surrounded by all these delightful acts of generosity.

Above all, the discipline of not buying things gives me more time to spend doing the things I enjoy, rather than feeling the pressure of having to earn the money to keep up with the fashions. The consumer world is very effective and persuasive. So we need the discipline of not buying things, in order to live what I suggest is a happier and more joyful life.

The last discipline I want to share with you is the discipline of silence. Silence is a great teacher. It allows us the peace and space for our deeper voices to be heard. We experience a wisdom that we normally miss through continual noise and busyness. In silence we experience more beauty, we see more clearly, we hear without distractions, and we feel our total experience. Therefore, we know ourselves more fully, making wiser choices from the place of knowing truly who we are and what makes us most content.

All these disciplines have led me to feel freer and happier. Yet so often I resist what I know is good for me. Take exercise, for instance. I know I enjoy it, and feel better for doing it, but I generally resist getting out there and doing it. Or, when I have a choice between eating something healthy or devouring a cream and jam doughnut, which really does me no favours, I go for the doughnut. Why do I resist eating the healthy option? Well, it's a habit. But with the friend of discipline, and with awareness, and kindness, I can choose the healthy option, mostly.

18

Listening deeply

We need to allow space for our deeper thoughts to communicate with us, and for our body and heart to relay those deeper aspects of our inner world to our conscious mind. The deeper aspects often go unheard. Such communications can be very quiet and subtle; we need a keen ear and deep silence to hear them. Yet once practised at deep listening, we can do it anywhere, just by stopping, listening, and simply being.

To *listen deeply to yourself* you need space, free time, and being in nature; a willingness to listen and feel deeply, and then a willingness to allow those feelings to be heard. You could meditate, reflect, lie on the grass and look at the sky, sit in the sunshine, walk in the rain, or just do nothing. Doing nothing, especially, may appear challenging, but giving yourself permission to listen in this way will reveal endless gifts which will enrich your life. I have found these gifts to be of great importance, as they lead to a freedom beyond imagining.

For many years I just pushed ahead in life with hardly any introspection. I just did what I thought I was here to achieve and succeed at – climbing up the ladder of my professional life, earning more money, passing more exams, hitting higher targets for my employer, having lots of friends, a full social life, lots of holidays, two homes, and volunteering in my spare time. This was a whole lot to juggle and took a massive amount of pressure to keep going.

I could not stop. I had no idea that stopping would even be good for me: no one had ever told me about the wisdom of quiet, of listening to myself. For me to learn to be quiet and listen deeply, it took my physical body saying 'Enough,' and creating a 'dis-ease' which shouted so loudly that I had no choice but to go to my bed. As I explain in Chapter 1, that 'dis-ease' was a true blessing. I began to learn that who we really are is waiting in the silence of our innermost being for our presence to hear and activate.

The most harmful form of non-listening is the non-listening to ourselves. We look at our mobile phones, tablets, computers, televisions, or we have the radio turned on while we are not really paying attention to it. Most likely we are multitasking. Even if we think we are listening, we often have chatter going on in our mind at the same time, thinking about how to respond to this person, or worrying about that person, or planning the future.

If we are not practised at listening deeply, we can easily miss the gems of what we are here for, and one day wake up old. Then, in the quiet, we may hear a revelatory new voice, and know deeply that we have missed something very important, something that we were meant to do in this lifetime. Do we want to have regrets at the end of our life? Unfortunately, reflecting on much of what we truly think and feel can seem unacceptable to us. To some extent we have all been conditioned to deny our self-pity, anger, desire, jealousy, or our wonder. Most of what we take to be our adult response to life's painful events is no more than our unconscious decision to avoid listening to what goes on inside us.

As with any human relationship, not listening to ourselves damages our self-respect. It blocks the free flow of love within, towards ourself. Instead of being afraid or dismayed, we need the space to allow ourselves to feel, a space inside our hearts that's large enough to safely contain what we feel and hear, knowing that whatever arises is workable, necessary, and a gift. This is what any healthy human being needs to do. Sadly, we often fail.

Sometimes what we hear from within is difficult to work with on our own. We will need friends, or maybe even professionals, to help us steer a path towards the true wonder of this amazing being that we are now and always have been, a being which contains so much deep wisdom waiting to be heard.

To *listen deeply to others* you need awareness. Whenever your mind is occupied, usually quite unconsciously, with your own thoughts and plans and strategies and defences, are you aware that you are not listening to the other person? When you are not listening, you are not according them respect that is their due. They will know this instinctively and react accordingly. It doesn't take a psychic to know that someone is not really listening. We are so accustomed to not being listened to that we can take such behaviour for granted, even consider it normal.

Yet how startling and powerful, magical even, when we experience really feeling heard by another person! There is a practice called 'looping and dipping' that I would like to share with you. 'Looping' refers to checking out what another person has said; we do this by repeating back what we have heard, to make sure we have understood correctly. Without looping, we tend to hear through the lens of preconceptions, judgements, our own life history, and habits – also with emotions we bring from conversations with other people. Looping means we can check that we understand what has been said before we reply. 'Dipping', on the other hand, refers to checking in with ourself, to notice how we feel about what has been said. Only then do we respond.

Slowing down the process of listening by looping and dipping helps us to gain real clarity and perspective and makes life much simpler in the long run. Each of us has a desire to be listened to, and being heard certainly feels good: it's a universal need. For absolute health we need at least one person to whom we can say anything at all, who truly hears and witnesses what we say. It's not essential for that person to respond, such is the power and freedom of being heard.

So many people who commit suicide have not told anyone about how they are feeling, or have not been able to share their inner world with a dear friend or family member. It's vital for us to allow others to hear us, and for us to hear them. When you consider the problems of sexism, racism, ageism, classism, or homophobia, it's easy to see how they stem in large part from the fact that people are not recognized or heard, with tragic consequences throughout the world. Everyone wants and needs to be included in this human family. To be included means more than being equal under the law, more than having equal economic and social opportunity: it means being truly heard and fully understood.

To *listen deeply to the universe* requires what is called 'beginner's mind'. No one can be an expert on what has never been heard before – heard in exactly this way, at this precise moment. This kind of listening takes being ready to live this moment fully, and being willing to confront what is truly new, without preconceptions, without identities that need to be held up as barriers against what wants to come in. When we cultivate an 'I don't know' mind, we can stay completely open to any new possibility.

Because knowing gives us definition and control, it also enables us to keep the world at arm's length. Having established our ideas and preferences about reality, we no longer bother paying attention; 'we know'. We've fixed it all – but in fact we have closed ourselves off from the universe. Not knowing, instead, leaves us vulnerable and free. Not knowing is intimate, we are unprotected and fully engaged. By not knowing, we can merge with what confronts us. We can let go of identity and judgement and allow ourselves to surrender to amazement.

On a recent retreat called 'Simply Being', I was able to feel closer to the universe, freer of diversion, freer of distracting thoughts. The Welsh valley where the retreat was held was tranquil and quiet. As my mind began to become calm, and free of planning and strategizing, a real pleasure arose, then an astonishment, to hear the peep of a bird, the roar of a river rushing through the rocks, the crunch of gravel underfoot, the fall of rain, the wind in the pine trees, even falling leaves landing. I felt an intimacy with the living universe, along with its atmosphere of warmth and ease, pleasure and cosiness, without a need to prove or achieve anything at all.

Listening deeply, simply being, feeling connected to the surrounding universe, we can all experience details of ordinary life differently: they become extraordinary.

19

Imagination

We imagine all the time: without imagination we can't exist, we can't live our daily lives. We imagine what we are going to eat tonight, and whether the ingredients are in the cupboard. If we find they are not, we imagine the shop to buy the ingredients from. We then imagine if we can fit shopping into our day, and so on. We even have to imagine our way to the toilet. Our imagination is at work most of the time, and at night it's active in our dreamworld.

Often I hear people say, 'I'm not able to imagine, I don't have an imagination.' Well, we all have hopes, don't we? These are merely imagined pictures of the future; we all have memories, which are imaginings of the past; we all have fears, which are also acts of imagination. Each of our hopes, memories, and fears is an illusion, a story, yet seems very real.

As with what we dwell on, what we imagine – what we turn our heart and mind towards – we become. If we imagine with positivity and confidence that an outcome will be great, then set out on our mission with enthusiasm, even if it doesn't work out, we will have enjoyed our life in the meantime.

Hopefully, too, we may have learnt something that will help our future direction. If we imagine that things will go wrong, they generally will. Even if they go well, we have added unnecessary fear and pain to our life's journey, and overall this won't have helped the possibility of things turning out well. Imagining the worst usually keeps us locked into the pain of a limited, internal story. We can find ourselves choosing to be a victim of the past, at the mercy of other people's actions and thoughts about us.

When I was ten years old, I started singing in the local church choir. One day I was asked to try a solo. I had never sung a solo before and had received no training for it; I knew that my attempt at the solo was not particularly good. Yet instead of helping and supporting me to improve, the choirmaster and other boys made unhelpful comments and embarrassed me to the point where I chose to remove myself from the choir. Unknowingly, until I was forty-five, I held on to the story that I could not sing. Then, with a new awareness, I started to see differently, and decided to take some one-to-one singing lessons. I stopped choosing to fall victim to those words spoken by the choirmaster and boys. Deep down, I knew I was able to sing perfectly well – everyone can, if sufficiently supported, encouraged, and trained. I chose, therefore, to step into a new, positive experience rather than stay with the limited, painful story from my past.

This example relates to many aspects of life, some of which are far more painfully damaging. But there is always help out there, if we know where to look, and we can always change our mind. Imagining the amazing and the awesome can help our life positively and magically fly free from being held within the tight box of a life conditioned by unhelpful events from our past.

We are always stepping into a new future, new possibilities. In the words of Chapter 2, it's never not now; if I am present *now*, this moment, this second, is always new, one we have never had before. We can imagine a new perspective, a new and beautiful view. We can see differently. Doing so has a power and magic beyond our imagination. Positive, kindly energies from the universe will somehow join in to help bring about worthwhile projects, relationships, or events. Synchronicities and coincidences will happen more and more. It's as if you are in a positive slipstream, an energetic flow which is bringing about unexpected, delight-filled aspects of what you choose to imagine.

Since my personal growth journey started in 1990, I have received so much support from many people who are further along the path than I am. I have been given so many gems of wisdom that have helped me see through the illusions that create unnecessary pain, and enabled me to view things more as they really are. Now I can understand how I create my life: I create the second dart of my suffering (see Chapter 8), I create my joy, and I create everything in between. I can see that when I choose to imagine positively, this choice has a huge impact on my future.

So I have chosen to dedicate myself to becoming a force for good in the world. This sounds a bit grand, but having this imagined intention, this volition, helps me remember to give and love – and, like Cinderella, to have the courage to be kind and compassionate to all forms of life. I can choose to think about other people and other sentient beings, and about what they need. It's not about me, but if I can give, be kind and loving, and be truthful to others, then my life feels amazing, which really is a win-win outcome.

Many people's philosophy is based on greed, living from a fear of never having enough, the imagined future always worse than the present. They feel they need to have more, even if what they have now is absolutely fine. Another philosophy is based on hatred: taking power over others, judging others badly, pushing away certain people in society, cutting off and ignoring or even attacking others. This can give rise to wars, in the attempt to get rid of threats; more often than not threats are imagined, and blown out of all proportion by news stories and sensationalism. A third philosophy is based on delusion, which in fact creates the other two states of mind, greed and hatred. We think that if we have more, and get rid of what we don't like, then we will be happy. This is a wrong view, based on not seeing things as they really are.

If we could step into the shoes of others with compassion, and communicate with them, we would find that other people are just like us: they have their fears and joys, too. If we could understand others through our hearts and not through our fears, then many lives would not only be happier but saved. We would soon realize that we can love these people, not hate them. We could become aware that the joy of giving is far better than the greed of taking, and the desperation of always wanting more, never finding contentment.

The Buddha said that there are three poisons in human life. These are greed, hatred, and delusion. He said that the medicine for these poisons is generosity, love, and wisdom. Through watching myself and others practise the arts of being generous, loving, and trying to see with clarity how things are, I have learnt that imagination is essential to living a rich and harmonious life, one that feels connected to all that lives. By choosing to imagine being a force for the good of all of life, including the planet, my life and the lives of many others have become easier and more joyful.

Imagination is powerful. Be careful what you choose to imagine.

20

Seeing differently and accepting difference

Throughout history it has been blatantly obvious that human beings do not accept difference very easily. Generally, we will avoid those people whom we perceive as different to ourselves, or else we will attack them verbally or physically; if not, we might ignore them, or pretend they don't exist, which is just as harmful. Some – maybe most – of the world's worst atrocities have happened because people felt threatened by difference, although no open threat was literally present.

Human beings tend to have views that are fixed, views that say a particular group of people or a certain nationality, a particular individual or a certain religion, are 'bad'. Wanting rid of these people, in our mind we deposit them all in a box labelled 'bad' or 'threatening'. This is a barbaric way to behave. Yet it seems we have still not learnt that everybody suffers through this deluded way of thinking. I say 'deluded' because when I look at reality, it's clear that every individual is unique. If we could only accept difference, thousands of people who are killed every year in wars and terrorist attacks would not lose their lives to violence; myriads of people who are tortured or abused in some way would not suffer; countless people who commit suicide due to discrimination would be alive today.

We can really harm others by doing nothing but having a wrong view about them. When we can see our fellow human beings differently, and accept their diversity, society will be healthy, enriched. Seeing this way is in line with reality, with how things actually are, and it's the loving thing to do. No doubt you have heard someone say, 'If we were all the same, life would be boring, wouldn't it?' However, do we really treat others as we would like to be treated ourselves, regardless of the colour of their skin, their nationality, their sexuality, their religion, their age group, their individual ability, or their tastes?

Life is so much richer when the truth of our difference is appreciated and enjoyed. As long as no one is harming anyone, then enjoy the fact of difference: it's a gift that educates and expands our minds and hearts and connects us to each other. Millions of lives could be saved and an enormous amount of mental and physical pain and emotional anguish could be avoided. A radical shift in perspective is required; one which moves away from illusion and distorted views, towards right and perfect view. It's worth remembering that you could have been born with a different sexual orientation, or into another religious tradition; you could have been born in another country, and so on. So ask yourself, 'Do I find it challenging or complicated to accept the differences I see around me?'

People, groups, nations, are all fighting because of difference. So what can you do? Well, you can make a huge difference in your own life, by simply taking an interest in everyone you meet. Taking this interest will immediately expand your perspective on the world, making you feel empowered by knowledge, and connected to more people. You will also have a feeling of belonging. You will be happier because you no longer fear the unknown. When you really start to know the differences in people, and understand them, you can begin to fully appreciate the unique beauty of the fact of difference. You can learn to see differently, simply by turning your views the right way up, and seeing things as they really are, rather than through the lying lens of our preconceptions, judgements, and safe habits.

When I am attending our local Buddhist Group, I never know who will walk through the door. When someone comes in, I have a set of thoughts which immediately sums them up – this is what the judgemental mind does. Left to its own devices, the judgemental mind will rather grossly choose to like or dislike a person even before a word has been spoken. What threatens us most is not knowing. So I have made a practice of approaching everyone who walks in and welcoming them warmly. I include them, am interested in them, and introduce them to others. I'm happy to tell you that this practice has really broadened my whole experience. I have been rewarded over the years by friendships with many amazing people, from all walks of life, and of all ages, people I would never have established a friendship with had I not moved towards them. And I know deep down that I don't need to fear anyone, if my heart is open.

This is probably a controversial chapter for some, but I invite you with love, to stop, look, feel, and listen to the history of human civilization regarding prejudice against difference. Then stop, look, feel, and listen to your own current thinking and views in this area. Imagine a world which we had not labelled or divided or put boundaries round so fully. Wouldn't it be amazing if this planet was a single world-country, with everyone working together, and being fed and housed? If we could only change our view, from illusion to truth, from greed to generosity, from hatred to love, from disconnection to connection, then the amount of food that is wasted in affluent countries could be shared. The world would be a much more equal and kinder place in which to live and thrive.

If you choose to dwell on the views that are clear and based on how things are, then happiness and contentment are available to all.

Does this sound like an idealistic dream?
Or is it something that we can all work towards, one
step at a time?

If we get acquainted with our so-called enemy, we will no longer choose to be threatened by them: it's possible we might then like them, or at least not hate them to the degree that we want to attack them. Sadly, this is not yet the case. We live in such a complicated and divided world that millions of people do not feel secure and cared for, therefore they will strike out in their pain.

I would like to expand on the subject of labelling things. We all have an inbuilt tendency to label people and groups and nations. This is OK, but if we are unaware we then fix those people, groups, and nations in our minds, by making them fit whatever the label means to us. This doesn't allow for any change or flexibility – or deeper connection with others (read Chapter 6, 'I can't change').

For instance, when someone first meets me, they might ask where I am from, or what I do. I never answer that question by saying what I do for my work (the answer that's normally expected), because mentioning my work will box me in with a label. I tell the person about things I do for pleasure. This reply will still label me as a person who likes to meditate, or go to the cinema, and so on, but it shifts the perspective away from what can be easily labelled and feels more friendly.

When I was ordained as a Buddhist, I was given the name Danapriya. I have noticed that my Buddhist name can either connect or divide, depending on the other person's labelling system. If they are interested in difference, and concerned with me as a person, something magical can happen. We can learn from each other and enhance one another's perspectives. We can feel connected, although we may have different views, and practise in different spiritual traditions. Accept difference!

We live in a period when the world as a whole seems to have little or no long-term practical commitment to caring for the planet and its inhabitants, including us humans. Rather than acting from greed and hatred, to survive as a species, we need to make a unified and collective choice to take care of all life on this planet. This doesn't look likely to happen globally any day soon.

Most importantly, though, each of us can brighten up our own corner. This means me working on myself, and you working on yourself, to develop an evermore loving, generous, and connected outlook. By seeing differently, you will certainly benefit, and so will everyone around you. Learn to see differently by accepting difference.

21

Other power and consciousness

If you really pay attention, you don't have to live for a very long time without experiencing the feeling that something else is going on in the universe beyond ordinary logic or reason. Children can be particularly aware of another energy existing alongside us, but this sensitivity can continue. Take ageing, for example. I certainly see my physical body ageing: my hair has changed colour and fallen out, I have aches, and now the odd wrinkle has appeared. Yet my consciousness and inner life of thoughts and emotions don't seem to have aged in the same way. Internally, I feel the same as I did thirty or forty years ago. This makes me think that the body and consciousness are separate. They have different characteristics. At death, the body returns to air, water, fire, and earth – the basic physical elements of which it is made – but I get a strong sense that consciousness then flies free and transforms into something beyond.

Actually, I don't know. We can't know. The longer I live, however, and the more I tune in to the positive, kindly energy that I experience in the world, the more my life seems to progress smoothly, and the more 'coincidences' seem to happen with more synchronicity. This can't be my imagination, since it's my actual experience. Each of us can only make sense of our own life from our experience.

In addition, the more I ask this other energy, or power, to help me be a force for good in the world, the more I notice unusual things happening that are helpful for me and for others. I know many people who have these types of experiences as well. Now I'm not talking about God, although others might, to make sense of their experience. I truly believe that the help others receive from their religion and their faith in a deity can't be different from what I am talking about: it's just that they label it differently.

I don't want to name this 'something beyond'; for me, to limit my felt sense of it by referring to a doctrine is not helpful, because none of us honestly knows. This is a dilemma for us human beings, as we want to pin things down and know them rationally. What I am talking about here is unknowable in our customary, rational way of making ourselves feel comfortable, which may lead to a blind faith. In this chapter I am sharing a few experiences that have led me to believe in something else, something that feels kindly, and which is beyond our usual understanding.

For most of us, our mother's death is a significant life experience, whatever the state of the relationship. My Mum died on 3 April 2012. In my case I was shocked into a slightly altered state of consciousness, a state that grief can sometimes create. Six days after Mum died, I was sitting in the shrine-room at the London Buddhist Centre, listening to a talk along with about sixty others. Part way through, I glanced around the room to see who was there, and became aware that Mum was standing in the middle, smiling at me. She was wearing navy trousers and a pink, white, and blue blouse that I recognized. She had had her hair washed and styled (having her hair done was one of her pleasures, which she had enjoyed every week throughout her life).

Mum stepped gently over someone, bent down and looked into their eyes. Then, standing up and looking back at me, she said with a smile, 'Aren't they lovely people!' She repeated this twice more, stepping somewhere else, bending down and looking into someone's eyes, all the time smiling at me with great emphasis and saying, 'Aren't they lovely people!' Her image then dissolved. What happened? I have no idea. As far as I know, no one else saw what I clearly saw, yet the experience was as solid and as real as any experience I have in everyday life.

Another experience: writing this book. I never considered myself someone who would be able to write a book. The word 'book' seemed too big and ambitious, suggesting an impossible task for me. Yet the person I look up to and respect most in life said to me, 'Well, you didn't think you could start a Buddhist Centre, but you did, and it's thriving eleven years on.' So I was inspired to start writing the first chapter.

I told a friend about my idea for a book. He and I meet regularly to talk about aspects of our spiritual life, to help each other. (I know I can't do this journey alone, and I need others' perspective and help.) He said, 'Oh, I can tidy up the English for you.' 'Wow,' I replied, 'that's wonderful.' I sent him a roughly written first chapter, and when, after a couple of days, it arrived back in my inbox, I read it through. How amazing, I thought, that I can write a rough outline of my thoughts and ideas and they will be returned in marvellous shape! This inspired me to continue writing and to believe in the book. After writing two chapters, I thought about contacting a publisher. I telephoned one and explained that I was completely new to being an author, and wondering when I should ask a publisher to be involved. He asked me some exploratory questions, then became very enthusiastic, saying, 'This is exactly the sort of book we are looking for someone to write just now!'

I needed to think about promoting the book. I felt a bit scared about all the technological aspects of engaging with social media but wanted to set up a YouTube channel showing weekly ten-minute excerpts from this book. A few days later, while having supper on retreat with people from all over the world, one of them said to me, 'I can help you with the social media and the YouTube channel.' Throughout the adventure of making this book, the coincidences and synchronicity have been extraordinary. When they happen, I feel I am in a flow, and that when I focus my energy on something that will be of positive help to other people, some other power joins in.

Cast your mind back: have you had any similar experiences in your life? Here is one more example from mine. Recently my partner and I decided amicably to stop being partners, a relief for both of us. Our time as partners had been great for two and a half years, but had had its season. Before we changed our relationship back to friendship, we had planned to live together and buy a house, so I had put my flat on the market. It was for sale for over a year, but didn't sell. We couldn't understand why; the property was well located and in good order, and the price seemed right. After my former partner and I had decided not to buy a house together, a potential buyer made an offer on the flat within four days! Had it sold earlier, our parting would have been much more difficult.

Something in the universe seems to know better than I do. Over the years I have learnt to trust it. I let go and enjoy whatever happens. Of course, each experience of this kind could be a coincidence – but choosing to live in touch with this other state of consciousness and believing in this other power, whatever that is, makes my life much more magical and wonderful. Trusting in this way means we can more often let go of the fear, anxiety, and worry that can make us feel as if our lives are being strangled. It's not the fear, anxiety, and worry that strangle us, but choosing to live this way.

Stop, look, feel, and listen to reality and to your experience. Your senses are your communication with the universe. If you don't stop and tune in to them, don't feel them, don't note what your mind is up to and how your emotions are changing, then you will go through your life blind, numb, and unaware of the life you are meant to live. You will miss what brings most joy, ease, and wonder. Your inner awareness has all the answers. The information is always with you in the humanness of your being; you don't have to google anything. Or even read this book.

So stop, look, feel, and listen: become aware of what is. Then you can make wiser choices. Only you can decide. It's fine to listen to others, but they can't really know you as you know yourself. Open up to the possibility of another power, a kindly energy, a force beyond the personal. Since I was a child, my experience has consistently been telling me that there is some amazing help available, if I can but ask for it. You, too, could ask, and see what happens.

Whether all this is true doesn't matter to me in the least. I would far rather live in a world infused with imagination, beauty, and magic, than in a fear-ridden world of negative thoughts, disaster news, and narrow perspectives. The universe is huge, mysterious, and largely unknown. We can all embrace it with helpful and positive imaginings – or are they imaginings? My experience over the past sixty years tells me they are not. Remember, your life is what you dwell on.

22

The great value of facing our own death now

From one culture to another, death is viewed very differently. I don't know if you are from a culture that really celebrates a person's life and doesn't hide the truth of death, or from one which almost pretends death doesn't happen. Some cultures honour and respect an individual's life; this can help heal the grief of those who were close to the person who has passed on. Other cultures tend towards not talking about death, often because people are embarrassed and don't know what to say. If you are the person grieving, others avoid you or are awkward around you. This feels terrible but is common in my home country of the UK.

Do you know that, in the UK, anyone can lead a funeral? Yet funerals can be impersonal affairs: the celebrant may never have met the deceased. The ceremony may feel cold and anonymous, the life and spirit of the lovely person who has recently died not at all present in the atmosphere. This happens, I suggest, because people feel uncomfortable with facing or even thinking about their own death. A huge number haven't even written a will.

So try to leave people well, because you don't really know if you will see them again. Coming to terms with the truth that one day, maybe even today, you will die, will enhance your life rather than impoverish it. This is in no way morbid. In fact it's morbid *not* to face your own death as a reality. Then you would be living as if you were only half alive. Why?

When you live each day as if it's your last, you make every moment count. Every interaction matters and your experience has a new vividness. You leave everyone well, as if you may never see them again. You have no grudges against people. You leave no kind or loving thought unsaid. Does this sound like a fairy tale? We celebrate the excitement and wonder of birth; so why not celebrate the beginning of each day of our life as if it's our last? One day *will* be the last day, but we don't know which day that will be. Therefore, revel in the beauty of each amazing day: the rain that sustains us, the sun that supports us, the wonder of nature, the joys of family and friends, our home, and all that's part of our wondrous life.

If we don't live in this way, we can end up fearing death, pretending it won't happen to us, or only when we are ninety. But even ninety years will whizz by! If we have not made the most of our time whilst alive – if, instead, we have put things off, used unkind words, not spoken to people that matter to us for years because of a small disagreement, lived as if we have forever – then the quality of each moment will look grey and opaque rather than shining with bright colour. In short, we will have lied to ourselves.

Here is a practical question: have you written a will? A surprising number of people haven't. This is another task that tends to be put off to another day, because you are not going to die yet, are you? I found writing my will a joy. I understood that making a valid will is an expression of care for those we love and those who matter to us. It's also about not leaving a mess for others to sort out when they are dealing with the grief of our death. They won't need to guess what we would have wanted.

I expect you feel you have worked very hard for things you own and cherish. So spending some time thinking about generosity, about whom you would like to enjoy your material possessions, your money, and your home once you have passed away can be hugely rewarding in itself. I have also written down what I would like for my funeral: the location, who will lead the ceremony, and what music and readings will be performed. I don't want people to wear black, and I would definitely like lots of colour and balloons: I want a celebration. I enjoy my friends, my family – my life, with all its ups and downs, joys and pains. This is why Chapter 1 is called 'Even pain can bring blessings'.

I review my will and funeral wishes every two years or so, as circumstances change, people die, loyalties shift. I continue to reflect that all of life is change. I keep a copy of my will on the computer. I substitute a few names and numbers and mention certain gifts for certain people. Then I print the document and ask two witnesses to sign it. The job is done in about an hour, and costs nothing.

So even if you answered 'Yes' to the practical question, it may be a good idea to ask yourself whether you need to change your will. The people you care for and love, are they worth it? When you are talking with others or writing to them, remember to let them know that they matter to you. They or you could die soon, or either of you could suffer an accident that makes communication impossible. And if none of this happens, then your relationship will certainly be more loving and real.

By having the courage to think about your death now, you will see the colour, emotion, and wonder of your life become much more vivid. I have heard that, after a near-death experience, people become aware of two things: wanting to love others more, and wanting to evolve, develop, and learn more. They want to focus on compassion, love and wisdom, learning and evolving. So live every day as if it's your last.

23

Complexity versus simplicity

Some of you may remember the time when most households had just one telephone connected: it was a landline, and the telephone service was provided by a single company. These days it's not uncommon for almost every member of a household to own a mobile phone, and often the home still has a landline. Meanwhile, choosing a telephone service provider has become very complex if you want 'the best deal'. Once you have chosen, the contract lasts twelve or eighteen months, and then your costs are likely to increase if you don't go through the process of researching and choosing a new contract. In the UK it's the same with the gas and electricity suppliers, and with bank savings accounts and their interest rates. Also, in the past, when a customer stayed with a provider they were rewarded for their loyalty and supporting that company. Nowadays *new* customers tend to be rewarded, exerting yet another pressure to switch to new contracts and companies.

Of course, there are good and helpful aspects to having such a wide choice. Yet the same wide choice can make life more complex, potentially more stressful and anxiety-provoking. Are we choosing to add frustration to our lives?

Until the 1990s, there was just one railway company in Great Britain, which offered a simple set of fares. I know this, because I used to be a travel agent and sell railway tickets. Today, especially if you want a good deal, buying a train ticket can be very tricky. I always feel as if I am being manipulated by the websites to purchase the most expensive tickets online. With patience I can search around the numerous train companies and look at buying single tickets or breaking the journey to gain savings, but this requires more time, and is more complex.

In so many areas, it seems that variety has become extreme, and adds complexity. This can take us away from experiencing our lives at a deeper level. Daily life can so easily become a matter of list after list of things to do, in order to keep rethinking our choices as customers and consumers. Such juggling can create the feeling of the oppression of time. What we do with our mind in relation to this complexity will make all the difference.

If you have a television at home, you may not know how many channels are now available for you to watch. People say they can't be content watching a particular television programme, because there may be something better they haven't found yet, on one of the other hundreds of channels that their subscription may offer. They keep channel-hopping, which is exhausting, and a habit which I suggest doesn't go far towards creating a happy or a contented life.

I must admit to being a fan of television soap opera. I used to watch so many, feeling that I couldn't miss an episode. Since I couldn't record them to watch later, my daily life would revolve around 'getting in front of the box' when the serials were showing. Then I went on my first retreat, where I started to reflect on aspects of the way I spent my life. On retreat I enjoyed having the time to do simple things: walking in nature, talking with like-minded people, meditating. I felt easier and somehow happier. I found I was not missing the time pressure of spending all those hours watching soap operas.

Once home after the retreat, I soon switched on the television. An advertisement appeared, for a telephone service provider: a woman is sitting on a sofa, her attention totally absorbed by her favourite television programme. When the landline rings, she is angry about the interruption. Grudgingly she answers with a 'What do you want?', before realizing that the caller is a good friend. Then the woman is seen lying on the sofa laughing and talking, while the soap opera plays in the background, and the logo of the telephone service provider appears on screen and says, 'Be in your own life.' It was then that I woke up. Suddenly I saw that watching all those hours of television each week was not my life, nor was it the actors' lives: soap opera dramas are all made up!

There and then I decided to get rid of my television, and I haven't owned one since. Such decisions create space – they make life simpler and more real. I chose to be in my own life, to have time to do things that enrich each day, and to enjoy more space. (Of course, the challenge to keep making this choice has reappeared with such things as iPads and YouTube.)

My practice is to try to choose just once. A few years ago, I decided to find an eco-friendly renewable energy company to provide my gas and electricity, and then chose to stay with that company. Simple. I regularly need clothes washing powder, so I have chosen one to use, and stay with this choice. I avoid getting sucked into the complexity of revising decisions when grocery shopping; I escape the pressure to look at all the alternatives each time I need to buy an item. If you wish to experience simplicity and peace in your life, I encourage you to make each choice just once.

Every one of us strives for happiness and wants to avoid suffering. If you recognize that, then look to simplicity and see how you can simplify your life. Complexity will usually add to suffering, and therefore to unhappiness. Unclouded by the storms of complexity, simplicity can lead us back towards our deep inner voice, our inner knowing, our heart and compassion – to the space within us that knows.

24

Nature's message

I usually start my day sitting in a chair and looking out at the garden, observing the flowers, grasses, bushes, and trees, watching their stillness and beauty, noticing their states of majestic presence. Even if the west wind is blowing, the plants stand their ground and wave gracefully, which has a reassuring and calming effect on my mind.

Trees and plants take from the earth just what they need, no more, no less. In return they help all of life to breathe and provide a home for birds and insects and such tree-loving mammals as squirrels, koalas, and monkeys. Many trees and plants easily and naturally provide a source of food for a wide variety of life forms and help keep the planet's ecosystems healthy.

I always experience delight while sitting and watching the birds dart between the bushes and trees, as they find and share food. Their young are fed mouth to mouth, and as they drink or wash in the water, send a spray in all directions. The birds have no cares or worries, boundaries or concerns about who owns the garden, the house, or the land. Migrating with the seasons, carried by the airstreams, they are free to fly and roam wherever they will, without need of a passport, security, or control over which country they can visit. They have no home mortgage, money stresses, or need to find 'the best deal' – no becoming lost in thought, and no being over-rushed.

Watching the birds, I get a sense of the homeless life, the so-called 'going forth' from worldly concerns. The Buddha did this in India about 2500 years ago. He was among many spiritual seekers who left their homes to find physical and mental space, to commune more deeply with themselves and others, and with whatever is beyond the seen. These seekers were greatly respected and revered and given food and shelter during the rainy season. The homeless life was considered a completely positive way of existence back then. Nowadays we can look rather suspiciously at people who roam around the streets, although they, too, might be looking for freedom to ponder nature, the universe, and the meaning of life.

Nature is effortless. The seasons flow, winter into spring, summer into autumn before transforming into winter, each season having a spirit and mood of its own, if only we have the awareness to notice. Some people feel happier in one particular season than in another. Nevertheless each season holds a strong message for all of us: the new growth and excitement of what is to come in spring; the abundance of beauty, riches of food, and the warmth of summer; the thoughtful mood as the leaves float gracefully towards the earth in autumn, leaving bare branches while the leaves die back into the earth, to allow new life in the future. Then everything rests in the dark months of winter, restoring, recharging, nurturing, breathing quietly with absolute stillness as if nothing is happening. Yet this profound sense of nothing happening is essential for the bursting forth of the next, new spring as the circle of life flows on.

Hopefully these words are triggering thoughts about your life in relation to nature. Do you have a wintertime in your life when you stop and recharge? You may go away on holiday, but travelling can be as tiring, in a different way, as our everyday lives. I often hear people say after their holiday that they need another one to recharge! This is not always true, but so often we can want to be doing something on holiday, distracting ourselves from being still and nurturing our being. Even if we are lying on a beautiful beach, with the amazing ocean right in front of us, we can be reading or listening to music, or both. These activities together may seem restorative, but I suggest that on a deep level they are not.

Mostly, I get much-needed nourishment of body, mind, and soul by going on a solitary retreat. Admittedly, when I mention a solitary retreat to people, many can't understand why I would want to take this time alone to reflect, meditate, and be present in nature. Plenty of people don't want to be alone or feel unable to be alone. This is deeply interesting in itself, since we are born alone, we die alone, and in between we are alone even when with others. A solitary retreat truly enables the gift of getting to know ourselves, the time and space to stop, look, listen, and feel, and be aware of our environment, aware of nature speaking its message of a simple yet profound, harmonious existence.

In the UK there are many venues purpose-built for solitary retreat in beautiful locations, such as woods, countryside, by ponds and rivers, and up mountains. In these places I am out of the way of the hustle and bustle of everyday life, and unlikely to be disturbed by passers-by. I am without all my usual supports, including other people; I turn off my electronic devices, to be without these distractions. And whilst on solitary retreat I have experienced some of the most contented, ecstatic, and insightful moments of my life. Everything drops away. A freedom, an ease, and a beauty beyond the everyday arises out of a deep communing with nature, and with myself.

The weather takes on a great significance, the clouds, the sun, rain, wind, and temperature, as I become attuned to its moods, all of which are gifts for the planet, the universe, and space. When I contemplate the sheer size of the cosmos, the distances to the planets and stars, the earth's speeding around the sun every day, how the moon controls the tides and appears to change size, I find the scale mind-boggling, thrilling, and deserving of reflection as well as gratitude. The harmony that exists amazes me. The planets' relationships with sun, moon, and sea, the weather systems, the myriads of galaxies and stars, 'Wow!' We can learn so much from stopping, looking, feeling, and listening to this much bigger perspective – nature's message.

Of course, we humans are part of nature, too. Are we living in harmony with nature, or does our lifestyle create disharmony for ourselves and others?

Am I at ease with myself?
Do I create too many boundaries and walls?
Do I create too many rules?
Do I nourish myself on all levels?
Do I restore and recharge?
Do I spend time on my own in nature?

Nature's message

Do I notice nature's message?
Do I let nature touch my heart and spirit?
Do I let nature help me to see differently?

I know that when I am troubled by something, I can see it from a new perspective if I remember to immerse myself in nature, whether by lying on the beach, sitting in the garden or park, walking along a river or canal, or sitting up a tree looking up, down, all around. Even half an hour alone in nature can make the difference.

Nature's message always helps and guides, calms and settles. Clarity appears as if by magic.

25

Meditation helps all of the above

Over the past twenty-four years, meditation has enhanced every aspect of my life. Except sometimes when I am unwell or on holiday, I continue to meditate daily. Having taught hundreds of people to meditate, I have witnessed many lives changing positively through the greater clarity and awareness gained through meditation. By stopping, looking, feeling, and listening to ourselves, our inner world, we see what actually is, rather than just our story about what is, which always clouds reality.

Meditation is simple. Mostly we just need to sit quietly, be still, and watch our mind. The practice is not about stopping our mind, but about getting intimate with it – intimate with our heart's wishes and our soul's deepest needs. When we sit with ourselves and with what is, aspects of ourselves are revealed as the gifts of our inner wisdom and natural compassion slowly appear out of the mists. We can make wiser choices, because we can see more clearly and are more in harmony with our emotions and deeper volitions. This all helps create the life we are here for, a life that is evolving rather than devolving.

We can see through the unhappiness created by human

greed and hatred and notice our habit of being hoodwinked by the opinions of culture and other people. We can truly and deeply know what our own view is; as a consequence, we can see the trajectory that our life has been taking until now. We can reassess our life's direction, choosing with clarity the way we wish to go in the future, holding a view that truly mirrors the good in ourselves, good which is equally in all of us. In this way we can allow our unique gifts to nourish the world.

I am convinced that once we are aligned with our strong yearnings, and in harmony with wisdom and compassion, abundant energy unleashes heaps of positivity. That then flows towards us, up from our roots, down from the heavens, and out into the world, as a positive force for the good of all. A sense of belonging comes into being, a feeling of contentment, as if all our energies are integrated and going in one direction, in the right direction for each of us right now.

One of my friends once said, 'We are all just a mess in motion.' I laughed, because I could feel this to be true. You can have a bundle of inner selves with different people on duty at different times, like a collection of characters with diverse wishes and yearnings. One day you are ardently on a diet and choosing to eat healthily, feeling good about your discipline and the nutritious food you are giving yourself. The next day you can be eating too many sweet treats, making yourself feel physically unwell and, later, upset with the self that weakened. Later again you can be making a new decision to diet. And so it goes – such a cycle occurs in so many aspects of our lives. Meditation can greatly help to unite all the selves to become one amazing person who is travelling in one direction and creating an awesome force for good in the world.

Through meditation we start to see the things that truly make us happy, such as loving-kindness, generosity, truth, clarity, and living an ethical life. All the positive qualities, words, and actions help us to live with a clear conscience. Nothing weighs on our mind, our mind becomes still, the meditation can deepen. In this state of mind, we can gain further insights into the truth of existence and into what lies beyond our usual understanding.

On a more everyday level, I find that having a daily meditation practice makes my life go more smoothly. For me it works best to meditate first thing in the morning: the practice helps to set me up for the day, which definitely goes better if I have meditated. On those rare occasions when I don't meditate, the day can seem more jagged. I normally start by reading something inspirational or moving, such as a beautiful poem, and letting it have its effect as my emotions engage. I follow this with some exercises that help me bring my mind and body together and feel more present, before meditating for about forty or fifty minutes.

I get up early, but because I eat well and exercise regularly, I sleep well and more deeply, needing less rest and waking up early and bright. This routine enhances my life no end, I seem to glide into the day. I am more mindful and appear to have more time, and everything feels a little more spacious. When difficulties happen, which, of course, they do, I have the mental and emotional space to choose how to respond, enabling a more creative, less reactive response. This makes a huge difference to my experience at the time, as well as to my future. I feel I am effective and achieve *more* rather than less.

Many people imagine that if you are calm and relaxed and have a feeling of spaciousness, you will not get much done, whereas if you are pushing yourself, feeling pressure, and running everywhere, you will get more done. I suggest this is an illusion. In that over-rushed mode you are likely to make more mistakes and have to redo things, which will take up time. Also, you can make rash decisions when under pressure, making you less effective, and so much stress doesn't help your life at all. Which state would you prefer?

Meditation has helped me to experience my pain and find the blessings of a new way forward. Meditation has helped me see that it's never not now; therefore, I don't miss the ever-present opportunity of my life quite so much. Meditation has helped me appreciate the rich life I live, because of so many other amazing human beings around the planet doing things for me. Meditation has shown me that happiness is not out there – in fact it's inside me.

Meditation has shown me a different perspective on time. Meditation has taught me that I can always change. Meditation has shown me that what I dwell on I become. Meditation has shown me that I can get in my own way and then choose not to. Meditation has shown me that the true human condition is not lost in thought but knowing our thoughts. Meditation has shown me that I grieve to the degree that I have loved, and a life without love is not worth living.

Meditation has shown me that my speech can poison the atmosphere or it can perfume the air, the choice is mine. Meditation has taught me to have courage and be kind. Meditation has shown me that I need heroes and heroines who are further along the path of personal growth. Meditation has shown me that giving creates love. Meditation has shown me that I am stuffed full of love, and I can choose whether I let this love live.

Meditation has taught me that discipline is enjoyable. Meditation has shown me that listening deeply creates wisdom and compassion. Meditation has engaged my imagination. Meditation has helped me to see differently and to accept difference. Meditation has opened my consciousness to some other power, whatever that is. Meditation has shown me the great value of facing my own death now. Meditation has shown me the benefits of simplicity. Meditation has helped me to receive nature's message.

Meditation enables me to see things as they really are and find happiness and contentment. To try meditation for yourself, see www.danapriya.org for three practices led by me. Enjoy.

Epilogue

Now is the time to act

Thank you so much for reading my first book. I do hope you found some of it beneficial to you and your everyday life. While you were reading, I expect at times you felt inspired, and wanted to act – to make changes, evolve, and develop some aspect of your life. You probably touched on aspects of what is meaningful to you, what is important to you, and want to enhance your journey in this lifetime. Now is the time to act and make some choices.

After you put this book down, the energy and enthusiasm that the chapters have inspired in you will have dissolved within a few days. Our lives can be full and busy. We human beings tend to forget quickly; what is very important can slip away in the middle of all the distractions that we are choosing to be distracted by.

Most of us know a lot of teachings, a lot of wise words, and books like this one can bring them to the surface again. I encourage you: don't let what you know to be of great importance to you sink into the silt again. Then another chunk of your precious life will slip away, and not much will change until the next book, video, talk, or teaching and the cycle continues.

Act now.

Remember, discipline is enjoyable, and we need vigilance to stay present and engaged. To do this we need other like-minded people. We can't do it on our own. So if you don't yet belong to some sort of spiritual or personal development community, then I highly recommend you find one that resonates with you. Explore: there are many walks of faith, many spiritual groups, and many personal development movements. Depending on where you live, the number of communities can seem a little overwhelming or very limited. Just sit, go inside to your quiet depths, ask, then watch for the synchronicities. Magic may happen.

On the other hand, google, or find one friend who is on your wavelength. We so need the support of others, friends who are on a similar path that we can support and be supported by. The connection with these others adds so much more joy to our journeys and increases the likelihood that our efforts to grow and change will succeed.

If you haven't learnt to meditate yet – that is, learnt from a good teacher who has guided you – then I strongly encourage you to learn. Meditation develops awareness, and awareness is radical: it *will* change your life. To live without awareness is like being in a boat in the middle of the ocean, without a rudder or map, just being blown around by the worldly winds.

Go inside yourself, your map is in you, *it's not out there*. You then take full responsibility for your life. Grab your rudder tightly and with love. The responsibility for your life lies with you, no one else, no government, institution, or lover. You.

Stop, look, feel, and listen, and have the courage to be silent and alone. Don't be a victim to what is out there; if you are not careful it will be dragging you away from the essence of you.

Truly, what do you want to do with this precious life of yours?

WINDHORSE PUBLICATIONS

Windhorse Publications is a Buddhist charitable company based in the UK. We place great emphasis on producing books of high quality that are accessible and relevant to those interested in Buddhism at whatever level. We are the main publisher of the works of Sangharakshita, the founder of the Triratna Buddhist Order and Community. Our books draw on the whole range of the Buddhist tradition, including translations of traditional texts, commentaries, books that make links with contemporary culture and ways of life, biographies of Buddhists, and works on meditation.

As a not-for-profit enterprise, we ensure that all surplus income is invested in new books and improved production methods, to better communicate Buddhism in the 21st century. We welcome donations to help us continue our work – to find out more, go to windhorsepublications.com.

The Windhorse is a mythical animal that flies over the earth carrying on its back three precious jewels, bringing these invaluable gifts to all humanity: the Buddha (the 'awakened one'), his teaching, and the community of all his followers.

Windhorse Publications
info@windhorsepublications.com

Perseus Distribution
210 American Drive
Jackson TN 38301
USA

Windhorse Books
PO Box 574
Newtown NSW 2042
Australia

THE TRIRATNA BUDDHIST COMMUNITY

Windhorse Publications is a part of the Triratna Buddhist Community, an international movement with centres in Europe, India, North and South America and Australasia. At these centres, members of the Triratna Buddhist Order offer classes in meditation and Buddhism. Activities of the Triratna Community also include retreat centres, residential spiritual communities, ethical Right Livelihood businesses, and the Karuna Trust, a UK fundraising charity that supports social welfare projects in the slums and villages of India.

Through these and other activities, Triratna is developing a unique approach to Buddhism, not simply as a philosophy and a set of techniques, but as a creatively directed way of life for all people living in the conditions of the modern world.

If you would like more information about Triratna please visit thebuddhistcentre.com or write to:

London Buddhist Centre
51 Roman Road
London E2 0HU
UK

Aryaloka
14 Heartwood Circle
Newmarket NH 03857
USA

Sydney Buddhist Centre
24 Enmore Road
Sydney NSW 2042
Australia

Introducing Mindfulness: Buddhist Background and Practical Exercises
Bhikkhu Anālayo

Buddhist meditator and scholar Bhikkhu Anālayo introduces the Buddhist background to mindfulness practice, from mindful eating to its formal cultivation as *satipaṭṭhāna* (the foundations of mindfulness). As well as providing an accessible guide, Anālayo gives a succinct historical survey of the development of mindfulness in Buddhism, and practical exercises on how to develop it.

A wise and helpful presentation of essential elements of the Buddha's teaching . . . it will be of great value for those who wish to put these teachings into practice. A wonderful Dharma gift. – Joseph Goldstein, author of *Mindfulness: A Practical Guide to Awakening*

A gold mine for anyone who is working in the broad field of mindfulness-based programs for addressing health and wellbeing in the face of suffering – in any or all of its guises. – Jon Kabat-Zinn, author of *Meditation Is Not What You Think: Mindfulness and Why It Is So Important*

Bhikkhu Anālayo offers simple skilled mindfulness practices for each of the dimensions of this book. Open-minded practices of embodied mindfulness are described, beginning with eating and health, and continuing with mindfulness examining mind and body, our relation to death, and the nature of the mind itself. Significantly, by highlighting the earliest teachings on internal and external mindfulness, Bhikkhu Anālayo shows how, individually and collectively, we can use mindfulness to bring a liberating understanding to ourselves and to the pressing problems of our global, social, modern world. We need this more than ever. – Jack Kornfield, from the Foreword

ISBN 978 1 911407 57 7
£13.99/$18.95/€16.95
176 pages

Wild Awake: Alone, Offline and Aware in Nature
Vajragupta

'I had not met or interacted with a human being for weeks. I had just spent the night alone on a cloud-shrouded mountain. And now a fox and I looked intently at each other. …'

What is it like to be completely alone, attempting to face your experience with only nature for company? Buddhist teacher and author Vajragupta has been doing just that every year for twenty-five years. Here he recounts how these 'solitary retreats' have changed him, how he fell in love with the places he stayed in and the creatures there. He reflects on how the outer world and his inner world began to speak more deeply to each other, how there were moments when the barrier between them seemed to dissolve away. Also includes an 'A to Z' guide of how to do your own solitary retreat.

This is a seriously beautiful book (beautiful places and beautiful writing) – and I believe a wise one too. It will encourage (in the properest sense – 'give courage to') those who have longed for but have not dared to try out solitude – with its practical good sense, lack of self-indulgence and purity of heart – and also deepen the practice of those of us (Buddhist or otherwise – and I am otherwise) who already know the deep joys and freedoms, but also the harsh realities, of solitude in nature, in wildness. It is grounded in authentic knowledge and experience. Get out there – but take Wild Awake *with you.* – Sara Maitland, author of *Gossip from the Forest*

A fascinatingly anecdotal introduction to the practice of solitary retreat, encouraging us to go often and alone into the wild. – Kamalashila, author of *Buddhist Meditation – Tranquillity, Imagination and Insight*

ISBN 978 1 911407 18 8
£9.99 / $12.95 / €11.95
216 pages